THE CORE PACKAGE

The Instructional Design Library

Volume 21

THE CORE PACKAGE

Richard C. Mentzer
Equitable Life Assurance Society
New York, New York

Danny G. Langdon
Series Editor

Educational Technology Publications
Englewood Cliffs, New Jersey 07632

Library of Congress Cataloging in Publication Data

Mentzer, Richard C
    The core package.

    (The Instructional design library; v. 21)
    Bibliography: p.
    1. Curriculum planning. I. Title. II. Series:
Instructional design library; v. 21.
LB1570.M39   371.39'442   79-23416
ISBN 0-87778-141-9

Printed in the United States of America.

Library of Congress Catalog Card Number: 79-23416.

International Standard Book Number: 0-87778-141-9.

First Printing: March, 1980.

FOREWORD

When I first entered the field of instructional technology, the core package was the first instructional design with which I became acquainted and subsequently developed for a wide range of learning needs. Given the luck of the draw, I don't think any new trainer or educator, including myself, could have been more fortunate. The core package is a highly systematic, efficient, and effective design which incorporates many of the design principles which we know *work* for students. But, you won't gain this experience without trying it.

I continue to be a believer in the "lean" approach to instruction. Not only is such instruction more efficient, but also it places some major responsibility on the student. The core package embodies the lean approach in such a way as to maximize several such advantages for both learners and facilitators.

An additional feature which the user of this design will come to appreciate is the manner in which the design places the student in a position to control his or her instruction. In relation to this is the need for the student to utilize available resources. Students do, typically, make greater use of resource people in this design, including the teacher and other students. Hence, the interaction process is greatly increased.

Finally, some mention should be made of the opportunity which this design provides for integrating a number of disciplines together. It is, after all, a *core* package. Different subjects, heretofore taught as separate, distinct courses, can be integrated to show how one relates to the other.

Danny G. Langdon
Series Editor

PREFACE

The "Core Package" design, although a very effective and up-to-date instructional approach, is not a totally new idea. In 1926, R.W. Selvidge, a leader in vocational education, described in his book, *Individual Instruction Sheets,* how task-centered instruction provided practical application for seemingly abstract principles. He also extolled the virtues of "learning by doing" as the best way for maintaining the student's interest and involvement in the lesson.

The core package design discussed in this book is based on these two ideas about task-centered instruction. Although Selvidge and his associates recommended the task-centered approach for vocational (trade) education, today we can see a much more universal application in education and training.

In addition to using Selvidge's ideas for task-centered learning (not his words), the modern core package also relies heavily on the instructional devices he called "individual instruction sheets."

From these basic ideas has evolved the modern "core package," which has developed a few steps further to take advantage of some other ideas—performance objectives, individualized learning, learner control, and other contemporary design and programming techniques.

A special "thank you" goes to Dr. Robert Meran, my mentor, to whom much of the credit goes for developing the concept of the core package instructional design.

R.C.M.

CONTENTS

ABSTRACT

THE CORE PACKAGE

The "core package" design is an excellent way to organize almost any type of education or training into a task-centered learning scheme. This book explains how to go about doing that and why.

The idea is that tasks from a particularly interesting discipline become the "core" for instruction around which are programmed a variety of instructional items from other, perhaps not so interesting, but related, disciplines. For example, a course in auto-mechanics can also include items (course objectives) from math, science, reading, and even history. For the learner, many subjects which had once seemed unrelated and not especially relevant can now be integrated into meaningful and comprehensible learning experiences.

The term "core," as used in this book, has nothing whatever to do with the "core curriculum" concept which was once popular in some elementary and secondary schools. In fact, it can be quite the opposite.

The core package itself is primarily a learner's tool. The typical core package is a collection of "instruction sheets" prepared to help guide and prompt the student into and through each learning experience called for in a program. These instruction sheets are designed to only start the learner going in the right direction—the learner must do the rest. The core package, through these instruction sheets, is heavy on process and light on content. With this idea of process built in, the core package will put most of the responsibility for organizing and managing the learning activity into the learner's hands, where it seems to work best.

A well-designed and properly programmed core package creates a situation for the student where all the learning objectives and activities are clearly attainable; and, more important for the learner, relevant.

Relevance is increasingly important for today's students. There is a growing impatience with programs and learning activities that do not have clear and immediate pay-off for the learner. The use of relevant tasks as the core of the learning activity helps satisfy that need and, at the same time, makes it easier and more efficient for most students to learn theory, principles, concepts, and other "abstracts." For sure, students are more motivated to learn subjects when they can see a direct connection to the performance of the relevant tasks. In short, it is possible to "piggy back" a whole set of secondary learning objectives on some subject in which the student has high interests.

Relevance is the focus of the core package design, and through task-centered instruction, a unique integration of disciplines and learner-efficient activity can happen for any program.

THE CORE PACKAGE

I.

USE

The core package has been used in a wide variety of education and training programs for very diverse learner populations. This author has used the core package design in projects for Job Corps vocational auto-mechanic education, secondary industrial arts education, insurance claims analyst training, insurance sales training, book editor training, and Peace Corps volunteer teacher training. The learners ranged from the youngest of 14 years to the oldest of 75 years. They were college graduates and high school dropouts. Some were educated under the American style of education and others were not. Fortunately, not all of these people were in the same program. Not even the core package has the flexibility to handle *that* order.

Each project format required a unique set of instruction sheets, different guidelines to the learner, and a much different application of resources. The design concepts followed in each project, however, were exactly the same.

1. Around a single primary discipline (core) relevant to the learner, other related or associated secondary disciplines will be most efficiently learned as each secondary discipline item becomes important to mastery of the primary discipline.
2. The primary learner relevant discipline (core) defined as tasks will provide the best framework from which abstract ideas can be learned.

3. Task-centered learning activity promotes learner self-actualization and learner control.

There is every reason to think that these concepts are just as valid for other types of programs as those mentioned initially. As these concepts are discussed, the reader should think of the broad range of disciplines where they can be used and the variety of learners for whom they are suited. The need to apply these concepts may be identified in many ways, not the least of which is what you hear from students and teachers alike.

- "Why should I study science and math? I'm going to be a photographer, a real free spirit unaffected by technology."

- "When do I get to practice selling? I can't take another hour on this theory of insurance sales."

- "What can I do with all that art appreciation stuff, Blaah."

- "Sorry, young man, but I can't permit you to take the radio repair course until you pass general science (dummy)."

- "I'm going to be a playwright. Don't bug me about the history of western civilization."

- "I only like auto-mechanics and you can . . . . . . all those other classes."

- "I know what has to be done! Why can't I do it my way?"

To the person responsible for designing an instructional program, one of the prime reasons for using this conceptual basis and the core package is to develop programs which are more relevant to the learners. There are large numbers of learners in our schools and industry who are most willing to engage in organized learning activity when they can see the relevance of both the learning activity and the outcome. Malcolm Knowles (1973, pp. 35-36) described these people as "goal oriented" learners. He contrasted their learning style and needs with those who engage in learning activities for social purposes or simply for the enjoyment of learning.

These goal oriented learners also seem to be most effective and aggressive about their learning when they are confident they can, in fact, achieve their goals, and when they have some control over the learning experience.

A well-designed core package gets these learners actively involved in the subject and taking charge of their learning because they:

(a) relate to a relevant core discipline;
(b) always understand what the end-result will be;
(c) know very specifically what must be learned;
(d) have a clear picture of how everything to be learned fits together; and
(e) follow a process by which to organize, develop, and manage each learning experience.

Students in almost any learning situation should find learning easier and more rewarding when equipped with this perspective.

This author believes it is possible to organize a total school curriculum around a core package approach, crossing through all disciplines. More likely, a core package will be developed for a single course of instruction and will incorporate course objectives from one or two related disciplines. In industry, the core package is normally developed around a specific job and is not thought of as a way to achieve training objectives for other than those specifically supporting that job.

This chapter of the book will discuss the types of instructional systems where the core package can be used, the instructional purpose it can serve, and the specific instructional approaches with which it works best. However, before looking at these uses, it is essential to understand *the* basic design factor of all core packages, the "performance objective."

The effectiveness of the core package design stems from the unique relationship between the core discipline and the associated disciplines, and the link between these is formed by learner performance objectives. Each performance objective is the integration of a core discipline task with one or more associated discipline items.

Figure 1 illustrates the integration of core discipline tasks with associated disciplines "A" and "B." Added to core task #1 are items #1 & #2 from associated discipline "A" and item #1 from associated discipline "B," which form performance objective #1. In the right column of Figure 1, each performance objective (#1 through #5, and beyond) is formed by adding the associated discipline items to a core task. Notice that to form performance objective #5, however, there are no associated discipline items, so the performance objective is defined solely from the core task. The governing factor in the relationship between core and associated items will be the instructional intent which will be apparent as the use of the core design is explained.

Figure 1

CORE DIS. tasks	+ Assoc. Dis. "A" items	+ Assoc. Dis. "B" items	= Perf. Obj.
#1	#1 & #2	#1	#1
#2	#3	none	#2
#3	none	#2	#3
#4	#4	#3	#4
#5	none	none	#5

Note: Typical core package could have as many as 30 or 40 performance objectives.

Figure 2 shows an example of associated discipline integration in an automotive tune-up program:

Figure 2

Tune-up core tasks	Science items	Math items	Perf. Obj.
1. Gap spark plug +	1. Electron flow + 2. Compression & resistance	1. Decimal measures =	1. Set spark plug gap & test arcing under pressure to manufacturer's specifications (thousandths of an inch)

Instructional Purpose

Knowing the instructional purpose or intent for the program provides the key when determining what and how core tasks and associated discipline items are to be integrated into the performance objectives for a specific unit of instruction.

Typically, in the design of a core package, the performance objectives are written to one or more of three basic instructional purposes or intents:

1. To reinforce (establish) the core discipline tasks by adding to the learner's foundation or prerequisites necessary to perform specific core tasks. When the intent is to reinforce the core task, nothing is programmed into the associated discipline column that is not critical to the learner being able to perform that core task.

2. To illustrate or demonstrate difficult or abstract ideas in a familiar and/or an understandable context. Core tasks are used as a vehicle for the application of the important abstract core course objective and associated discipline course objectives. When using the core to teach the associated discipline course objectives, performance of the specific core task may not be a critical outcome.

3. To motivate student involvement in the associated disciplines through relevant high interest core task learning activity. When the intent is motivation, associated discipline course objectives are the most important part of the performance objective, and the overall core discipline and specific core tasks may only be a means of getting the learner to become involved in the associated disciplines.

The core package can achieve these different instructional purposes for the designer because of the unique way it pulls together the various disciplines (course objectives) around tasks that are in one way or another relevant to the learner. Once having identified the instructional purpose to be achieved, the designer must then define the core tasks and organize associated disciplines (course objectives) accordingly to that purpose.

The ability of the core package to deal effectively with these three basic instructional purposes makes the core package useful in almost any education or training system. Most instructional systems are weighted, although by no means exclusively, toward one or the other instructional purposes mentioned above, depending on the goals and objectives of the institution.

Instructional Systems

There seem to be three education and training systems that can use the core package effectively. There are two instructional systems (and associated institutions) with education as their primary goal and one with training as its primary thrust. The following is a brief description of the application of the core package in each system.

General Education

General education core packages are designed to assist students in achieving the stated general education goals of the institution or system. These goals are often expressed in subject matter disciplines, such as social science, math, language, and humanities, as well as disciplines we consider by their nature to be more task oriented, such as industrial arts, business, home economics, and the sciences. There are three things in particular that we might note about general education and the use of the core package:

1. The core package must be designed around task-centered subjects that have high interest. For many "goal oriented" learners, the courses that are by nature task-centered seem to be high-interest courses.

2. The core package in general education can be designed around any one of the many disciplines as long as that discipline has the range of tasks capable of illustrating defined course objectives and will motivate the learner to become involved.

3. General education is weighted to instruction that builds concepts, knowledge, and abstractions in each discipline, rather than specific skills. Tasks are not a particularly important outcome for the institution.

Within the elementary and secondary schools, industrial arts is a good example of a core discipline around which to achieve a wide variety of general education goals. Typically, when using the core package, the industrial arts class becomes the laboratory where many of the science, art, and language skills are applied. These are sometimes coordinated through a team-teaching arrangement when the core package is designed for wide institutional implementation.

Although not too practical in most general education systems, it is possible, for example, to design a year's curriculum for a student around the core package approach. In such a system, the learner, given his or her required performance objectives from the core package, could go to the assigned teacher in each associated discipline to draw up an individual one-year contract in that discipline. This would be based on mastery of the specific performance objectives with which they are integrated.

In the mid-1960s, there developed a number of Federal Job Corps general education programs designed totally around task-centered core disciplines. In these programs, all general education objectives were tied into a vocational core discipline.

More common today is the case of an industrial arts program within which the teacher builds the associated disciplines into the industrial arts instruction. Working with teachers from the other disciplines, selected course objectives from the associated disciplines are defined for inclusion into what would be the industrial arts core package. For this general education program, the specific industrial arts core tasks are probably not too important to the general education goals. For sure, not many general education objectives call for the cleaning and gapping of a spark plug by each student as a required performance. The associated discipline course objectives which can be selected out of other curricula, possibly for science, math, language, etc., are very common. In this type of general education core programming, the designer of the core package would "back into" each of the core tasks for identifying and analyzing all of the "real" course objectives to be achieved through the core.

Although industrial arts is a common example where core design is used to achieve general education objectives, almost any elementary or secondary school subject which can be organized into a task-centered program—and most can—will lend itself to a core design. Obviously, there does not need to be an associated discipline to use the core package. A single discipline can also be designed into a core package, if task-centered.

Vocational Education

Vocational education core packages are designed to prepare students for career situations in a core discipline by giving the learner a strong conceptual foundation in a limited number of associated disciplines.

The instructional intent of the vocational education core package is similar to that used in general education and is weighted heavily toward the illustration of abstracts. The core discipline tasks, however, are also important to the outcome. Vocational education programs prepare the student for work in a discipline "area" but normally not necessarily for a specific job or set of tasks.

The vocational education core package tasks are selected and included as representative operations of the real-world vocation. Each of the associated discipline items are selected to support the task conceptually, as a foundation, so the learner can deal with a broad range of similar, but not identical, tasks once out of the program and on the job. These associated discipline items might, as an example, still be science, math, language, etc., but this time they are carefully selected to strengthen the core discipline, if not specific core tasks.

In vocational education, the selections of associated discipline course objectives are not from the curriculum of another discipline, but rather are derived as a result of an occupational analysis within the core discipline.

Skills Training

Skills training core packages are designed to prepare a trainee for the performance of a specific job function or task.

The instructional purpose or intent of a skills training core package is, therefore, mostly to establish and reinforce the specific core tasks so they can be carried directly to the job.

To do this, the skills training core package is more tightly structured and programmed to the core tasks than that found in the vocational system. The learner leaves the skills training program with very specific skills to be applied to a well-defined job. The associated discipline items that are programmed into the skills performance objectives are totally supportive of the core tasks. Only after a careful task analysis of the core discipline (the job) and a definition of each of the required tasks are the associated discipline items determined. The associated discipline items in the skills training setting must be essential to the performance of the task, or they are not integrated into the performance objective.

Discussion of the Three Systems

The core package can be effective in each of the previously described instructional systems with careful integration of the disciplines to meet the goals of the system. In the general education system, the core is used primarily as a vehicle for achieving non-task course objectives.

For the vocational education system, the core tasks are considered as representative of the discipline in the real world and are primarily selected to best illustrate the abstracts of the core and associated discipline items needed to expand the core discipline concepts. In the vocational education system, the core tasks are only slightly subordinate to the associated discipline items and are equally important because both must be carried over to the world of work.

For the skills training system, the emphasis is closer on the core discipline tasks. In skills training, the core tasks are theoretically all that count in the final outcome. The associated discipline items are designed around each core task in order to get the learner to perform the core task.

No instructional program is so clear-cut as to be totally committed to just one of these systems. There will always be a mix of general education objectives in the vocational education programs and some vocational education objectives in a skills program.

Instructional Approach

Knowing how the core package is prepared for each instructional system and the instructional purpose it can serve, the final factor to consider is the instructional approach with which the core package works best.

The contents of the core package will be covered in detail later in this book, but to appreciate the instructional approach, the reader should know that almost every core package contains:

1. A definition of the terminal objective or goal. As an example for a skills training program, this would be an expanded job description.
2. A learning process for independent learning activity.
3. A checklist of specific performance objectives for the entire unit of instruction.
4. Various instruction sheets for each performance objective used to provide learning guidance and instructional prompts:
   - resources & references
   - general information
   - step-by-step
   - illustrations
   - exercises
   - tests

The core package is self-contained as a guidance tool providing organization and definition of the learning problem but does not usually provide complete content. The purpose of the core package is not to provide all the instruction but only to provide guidance and key instructional prompts which will keep the learner on track.

The core package can be designed to work with almost any instructional approach, from the traditional grouped classroom to independent study. There are two instructional approaches, however, served best by the core package; on-the-job training and individualized instruction.

On-the-Job Training

The learner is put on the job with an experienced worker who, in addition to regular production, is supposed to help the new employee (trainee) learn the job. Typically, that help goes like this:

> "Watch me, kid . . . working a case like this is simple . . . when you know the shortcuts."

The learner is right in the middle of the environment where everything to be learned is actually happening. The problem is, without some clear guidance, the employee cannot sort through everything. The work is not organized or managed for learning, nor should it be. The supervisor is neither a trainer nor program designer.

A core package designed for this "live work" setting will help the trainee organize and control the potential learning experience in that situation. The trainee's response to the experienced worker might be:

> "My training guide (core package) said that there are four steps which will help me understand the concept of that operation and the key idea is . . . Will you explain the four steps? I couldn't identify them as you worked the case. Could you elaborate on the key idea?"

The core package contains the guidance and prompting instructions to important concepts and the information necessary for the trainee to organize, direct, and manage the learning activity. The expert who is supervising the trainee on the job should provide models, monitor trainee performance, and give feedback at the request of the trainee.

When only a few people are to be trained in an organization, and the time and cost of special programs would not be economical, the core package in an on-the-job training scheme is often the most efficient approach. In fact, even after a trainee has been through a formal training program, the core package is an excellent way to make the transition from class to work.

Individualized Instruction

The facilities and resources for formal individualized instruction, as found in public schools, are usually organized for all the learning activities required by the student. The student is instructed individually according to his or her needs (within the capability of the class resources). The core package fits right in with this individualized approach. The student uses the core package with formal individualized instruction, much as the trainee does in the on-the-job training. Here, too, the student is guided and prompted by the core package, but in this individualized environment, the student has access to people and materials especially organized to facilitate the learning experience, which requires a different programmed core package.

In the formal individualized instruction, not only the student, but also the teacher uses the core package to manage the learning activity. The teacher constantly references the learner to the core package and monitors all the learning activity, not just the final performance, as might happen in the O-J-T technique. In an individualized instructional situation, this dialogue might be heard:

> "Yes, you are starting to get the idea behind performance objective #5, but it might help for you to read the textbook references cited on your instruction sheet for performance objective #5. After you've read those pages, let's discuss it."

The core package is an effective device with both O-J-T and the formal individualized instruction techniques. It is effective because it: (1) always gives a very clear definition of the required performance; (2) specifies learning activities; (3) provides key instructional prompts; and (4) includes a means for learning to be evaluated.

Summary

A final note on the use of the core package is that it is most effective at the basic levels of instruction with the naive learner who does not have a predisposed repertoire in the discipline. For more advanced levels, there may be more efficient approaches that require even less structured or programmed devices and rely more on process.

Use the core package approach: (1) for task-centered learning; (2) when instruction is to motivate students, illustrate abstracts, and/or reinforce tasks; (3) in general education, vocational education, or skills training; and (4) with on-the-job instruction or formal individualized instruction.

Reference

Knowles, M. *The Adult Learner: A Neglected Species.* Houston: Gulf Publishing Co., 1973.

II.

OPERATIONAL DESCRIPTION

The core package is a device designed and programmed to be used by the individual learner. If there are two students or 30 students in a program, irrespective of the instructional approach, each is to have a copy of the core package. The routine followed is basically the same in all instructional situations. The learner is given the core package and an explanation of how it works and is exposed to the learning environment until mastery of the objectives is complete. In practice, it is more organized and much more humane than a "survival" experience, but the idea is the same.

In 1967, this author heard Robert Mager say something to the effect that if learners are given a good set of objectives and put into the proper surroundings, they will learn as efficiently or, in many cases, even more efficiently than in a relatively programmed setting. The well-designed core package reflects that kind of thinking.

For the student, a core package specifies, guides, prompts (facilitates), and helps manage the learning activity. Much of the organization and management responsibility is shifted to the learner through the core package. For the teacher, it provides the opportunity to concentrate time interacting with the students on an individualized basis in immediate response to the students' learning needs.

Before discussing how the core package is used operationally, it is important to have a picture of the conditions required to make it work and a better idea of the basic components found in most core packages.

To make it possible for the learner to be more responsible and to free the teacher, the core package requires just the right kind of task-centered environment. Keeping in mind that the core package is based on "task" performances of one kind or another, it is critical that the learning facility be designed and equipped to accommodate each and every performance. Normally, for the O-J-T program, the environment of actual work lends itself to each of the tasks to be learned and subsequently performed by the learner. In the school setting, however, the conditions must be carefully designed and orchestrated to insure that learner performance can occur.

Examples of school facilities that are designed to accommodate the performance of tasks are a biology lab, cooking class, typing room, music room, machine shop, etc. These school facilities are usually organized for the learning activities to occur in what are called work stations, where each specific performance required can take place. Figure 3 is the layout of a facility specifically designed for the use of an automotive tune-up core package. Note that work stations are related to specific performance objectives.

In industry for O-J-T, the right environment is any place the desired learner performance occurs, such as at an editor's desk, in an insurance claims office, in the manager's organization, etc. In the O-J-T environment, the learner is expected to learn and perform the tasks as a part of the working facility.

In all cases, however, the environment must include the resource materials to support each and every learning activity in order to be efficient. Resources, such as manuals, books, illustrations, programmed materials, films, models, examples, and raw materials, can all be important. Most important,

Figure 3

Example of Work Stations

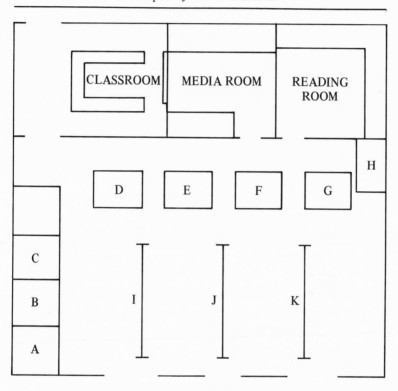

Performance Objectives

1. I & A	11. D	21. G	31. F
2. A	12. C	22. K	32. K
3. I	13. E	23. K	33. I
4. D	14. E	24. K	34. I
5. G	15. D	25. F	35. K
6. J	16. G	26. F	36. J
7. E	17. G	27. J	37. K
8. K	18. G	28. J	38. K
9. B	19. H	29. F	
10. D & C	20. H	30. F	

however, to the learner's environment are people who can expertly demonstrate and judge the performance of all the tasks expected of the learner and who are willing to help the learner whenever required.

The core package is dependent on the students being able to access resources and perform tasks, and the considerations for the environment are essential, whether in the structured education system or the live O-J-T system.

A core package is a limited and basic device of defined performance objectives, procedures for achieving the performance, and instructional subject matter prompts that will get the learner to use the resources to be found in the environment. It is normally not complex and, as seen previously, is made up of only a few components.

Most core packages start with a definition of the expected functional outcome to be derived from the program by the student. As an example, in a core package for an insurance salesman, the definition would center around the description of the salesman's job functions and skills as required by management. From this definition, the learner should know what the instruction will lead to and the perspective needed to enter into the program. In the core package, this is described as the learner's terminal objective for the total program.

Next in the package is a detailed and definitive checklist of performance objectives, such as those described in the first chapter. There might be as many as 30 or 40 performance objectives in a unit of instruction, all contributing directly to the learner's terminal objective.

The checklist is followed by an instruction sheet for each and every performance objective. This instruction sheet is usually referred to as either a job sheet or performance objective work sheet. This sheet is the main component for guiding the learner through a performance objective.

Following the series of job sheets, one for each performance objective, are other instruction sheets prepared to support the associated discipline items within the performance objective. Each associated discipline sheet is keyed to one of the appropriate performance objectives, and there are usually one or more of these associated instruction sheets for each performance objective. As an example, associated instruction sheets can take the form of programmed science sheets, math sheets, etc., depending on the associated discipline. There are other types of instruction sheets, such as the assignment sheet used for identification and discrimination exercises. Any instructional prompting the designer finds necessary to build into the package in order to get the learner to accomplish the performance objective can usually be programmed on the type of instruction sheets described here.

For most learners, this combination of materials is more than enough to facilitate a meaningful learning experience when coupled with the right kind of environment. The core components are not rigidly programmed. The whole point of the design is to be open and flexible enough for the learner to take the initiative—but defined enough to keep the learner on track.

There will be a detailed explanation of the core package content in the next chapter, but try to keep the basic components in mind as the functional operation is described.

In both the structured education situation and with the on-the-job training approach, the learner is normally given an orientation to the program that includes overall objectives, familiarity with resources, and a mental set about how to think of himself or herself in the system. The learner must understand his or her personal responsibility for the learning and his or her special role in the management of the system. Exactly what happens when a student starts the specific learning activity within the core package is important.

In every core package, the student is given an implementation process or routine. This routine does not prescribe what is to be learned; rather, it is a procedure that will guide the learner into the types of learning activities the designer of the package feels are educationally sound.

Most of what is built into the core package is process and not subject content. This is usually spelled out to the learner in terms of some kind of learning routine. For purposes of explaining an implementation routine, there are 11 typical steps which, given the proper environment, will provide the learner with the process necessary to move into and through each performance objective (PO).

1. Assignment (review of the performance objective).
2. Student planning (time, resource materials, people, facilities, etc.).
3. Organization (setting up for a learning activity for each specific PO).
4. Instruction (study job sheet and initial input).
5. Start task (begin performance objective tasks).
6. Exercises (from instruction sheets for specific PO).
7. Access resources (materials in support of instruction sheets and initial performance of task).
   - Readings
   - Models or examples of performance
   - Discussion group
   - Prompts and assistance from experts
8. Complete prompted task (finish task on job sheet).
9. Performance feedback (expert critique).
10. Remediation (more learning activities on deficiencies found in feedback).
11. Mastery (correct performance signed off by expert).

Although the routines for the learner in the formal education setting and O-J-T are basically the same, there is an obvious need for a different emphasis. As each of the 11 steps is reviewed here, keep in mind that learners working in the O-J-T system are almost totally responsible for organizing and initiating the learning activity. In fact, much of the real work environment can be unknowingly in conflict with the implementation of learning activities.

There is, as mentioned previously, an orientation to the entire unit of instruction prior to the application of the 11 steps. It is important to understand that the 11 steps are intended for the learner to apply to each performance objective and that the process is repeated for each performance objective in the program.

In the orientation to the program, the learner should review the program terminal objective, each performance objective, and the instruction sheets. The learner should know in detail what the outcome will be if he or she successfully works through the program. It helps if the learner discusses the terminal objective with someone who has completed the program to be sure the "goal" is completely comprehended and that the learner understands the relationship of the combined performance objectives and the terminal objective. Next, the learner should examine facilities and resources and identify generally where in the program they can be used. Finally, the learner should be instructed in the 11-step routine so that he or she has a process to use in attacking each performance objective, as well as a mental set for this process in order to manage his or her learning.

Orientation is more important for some learners than others, but it is critical that the learner know where the program leads to and how it works before being involved in the detailed learning activity.

Once orientation is complete, the student is ready to work on the first performance objective by following the 11-step process. We will now look at each step.

1. *Assignment.* The learner reviews the first performance objective and all materials in the core package which relate to that performance objective (job sheets and other instruction

sheets). From reading the core package materials, and if necessary by questioning resource people, the learner should understand in detail what the performance objective means and what must be done to successfully accomplish the performance objective. He or she must diagnose the problem.

2. *Student Planning.* The student must prepare a plan for accomplishing the performance objective. Looking at the job sheet, the learner can decide on how much assistance will be needed and which resources to use. Most plans will be based on the 11-step process and would include:

- reading reference material recommended on the job sheet;
- scheduling discussions with experts;
- seeing media or live demonstrations of task or examples of performance; and
- trying performances under supervision and asking for feedback.

After identifying required resources, time, materials, people, and facilities, a schedule would normally need to be prepared by the learner. This planning step forces the learner to be completely involved in the rationale of the learning process.

3. *Organization.* The student, with the help of the teacher (or supervisor), gathers together resources, sets up the facility, arranges for input from various sources (teachers, other students, outside resource people, etc.), and completes other necessary preparations.

4. *Instruction.* The student studies instructional information on the job sheet (instruction sheet central to the performance objective). There are several sections to a job sheet, but from an initial reading the learner should be prompted to explore other resources for more information, such as textbooks, references, other students, and teachers.

5. *Start Task.* The student should start the performance task whenever he or she feels ready. For some students, it means immediately, without any instruction. For others,

they may hold back until sufficient information has been assimilated. The student is encouraged to work on the task until he or she cannot go on and must turn to one or more resources for assistance. Usually, the learner quickly discovers his or her own best way to approach each new problem posed by the task. At this point, the learner should be reaching out for more resources. Each step in the job sheet procedure poses a problem and a learning experience. If the learner feels he or she has competency without instruction, he or she goes right to the performance feedback (step 9), and if the learner can demonstrate mastery of the objective, there is no need for additional instructional activity by the learner for that performance objective.

6. *Exercises.* Most core packages contain instruction sheets for each performance objective which are designed to draw in the associated discipline items for the performance objective. These are written with special exercises and problems for the learner's self-evaluation and to direct the learner's attention to key content points. If they work, the exercises in most cases will prompt the learner into accessing resources in an inquiring, problem-solving approach.

7. *Access Resources.* In support of the instruction sheets and the performance of the tasks, the learner will use the resources available. The use of a resource can be triggered by a specific reference in the core package, the learner's understanding of the problem, or the recommendation of the teacher. Some of the resources are:

- textbooks, manuals, operation documents, etc.,
- experts, other students,
- films, illustrations, and
- instructional program materials.

8. *Complete Prompted Task.* The learner completes the task defined on the job sheet using whatever resources and assistance are available. This initial performance of the task by the learner can be prompted as much as is necessary to get

the learner through the experience of completing the task, even though it may not be within the exact specifications of the performance objective. During this first experience, not the final one, the learner should be asking for demonstrations of the performance so that he or she can question and probe the experts.

9. *Performance Feedback.* When ready, the student performs the task unprompted. The performance is closely monitored by a teacher (or expert), who tells the learner things that are not done properly, explains how it should be, and possibly demonstrates correct performance afterwards. If the student uses no prompts and the teacher is satisfied that the performance was to the standards specified, there is no need for further instruction.

10. *Remediation.* If mastery of the performance is not demonstrated, the learner goes back to the resources and works on identified deficiencies until he or she can meet the standard of the performance objective. This may be self-imposed or suggested remediation.

11. *Mastery.* When ready, the student performs the task again unprompted and unassisted. The performance is monitored by an expert who "signs off" the performance objective for the student, if satisfactorily completed. In most core packages, it is literally a signing of the specific performance objective on a checklist.

After mastery of one performance objective, the student moves on to another. The student follows this routine or some other systematic process to achieve each of the performance objectives in the program. Learning routines or processes should be developed by the designer and by the learner to fit the particular situation. Any process is "right" as long as it allows the student control while maintaining valid learning activity.

The core package performance objectives, in some programs, are designed without a required sequence, so learners in a class will work on different objectives at the same time. For on-the-job training, where work does not occur in a totally predictable sequence, the performance objectives are designed to be somewhat independent of one another.

If there is no prescribed sequence to the performance objectives, the learner must be given additional guidance in the selection of performance objectives. Whether sequenced or random, the 11-step routine for accomplishing a performance objective can be used.

The core package, placed in the hands of the process oriented student and within a resource-rich environment, will be likely to get the student to achieve the program's terminal objective.

III.

DESIGN FORMAT

There are different core design formats as mentioned in the prior chapters, but all are prepared around task-centered learning concepts and the idea that the learner should have a great deal of control over the learning activity.

Every core package should be designed primarily as a learner's tool that will give the learner the ability to organize, develop, and manage the learning activity. There is a great deal built into a good core package design that makes this possible.

The core package gives a clear description of the program outcome, defines each required performance, guides the learning process, integrates learning content, specifies learning tasks, provides instructional prompts, and gives evaluation criteria.

All this, as discussed in previous chapters, is accomplished with just a few simple devices. The typical core package contains:

    (1) terminal performance description (defined outcome),

    (2) implementation routine,

    (3) performance objective checklist, and

    (4) instruction sheets.

This chapter will describe the design of each core package component and explain the design rationale.

For purposes of illustration, a core package designed for an automotive tune-up program will be used in this chapter. This illustrated core package was prepared for a vocational education/skills training system.

Terminal Performance Description

The terminal performance referred to in this automotive core package as the "program purpose" is illustrated in Figure 4. This is the description or definition of what the learner should expect as a result of successfully completing the program. It is the functional outcome the learner can expect for himself or herself and not a description of instructional activity. Also included in the definition are several qualifying statements which, in terms of the terminal performance, are as important as the tasks. In this example of a combination vocational education/skills training system, the occupational description, as well as the technical skill, serves to define the outcome. In reading this terminal performance description, it is apparent that both the core discipline of auto-mechanic tasks and two associated disciplines, in science and math, are going to be critical to successful performance. It is suggested that you read Figure 4 in some detail at this time.

If you are preparing a terminal objective for a non-occupational program, it, too, would still be expressed in terms of tasks and the relevant application for the student.

The learner should understand, after studying this terminal performance description and hopefully discussing it with an expert, just what the outcome from the learning activity will be. This complete "big picture" is important to establish before any detailed learning activity starts. With this perspective, the various isolated learning experiences should remain relevant to the learner throughout the program.

Figure 4

Program Purpose

Tune-Up Mechanic

After successfully completing the 38 performance objectives in this program, you will be able to perform the entry level function as described for a tune-up mechanic.

The tune-up mechanic locates, through analysis and procedure, engine malfunctions and determines services needed for the charging, cranking, ignition, and/or carburetor systems. The mechanic is able to read and interpret the proper diagnostic and measuring equipment to do the work.

The mechanic tunes automotive engines to exact specification; cleans, adjusts, and tests spark plugs; inspects and adjusts points; checks and adjusts ignition timing; sets valve tappets; replaces defective coils, condensers, and electrical connectors; removes, cleans, and assembles carburetors; tests and replaces fuel pumps; and tests batteries, connections, electrical charging and starting circuits, and replaces components.

The tune-up mechanic prepares cost estimates for customers and completes service orders.

Applicants for tune-up work must have the conceptual understanding of engine system operation to be able to perform tune-up tasks on a wide variety of automobile engines. An applicant must also be able to perform all mathematical computations and measurements essential for diagnosis and adjustments.

The tune-up mechanic is usually employed in automobile dealerships or in general automotive repair shops, where he or she works by a standard flat rate per job or at an hourly rate against the flat rate book performance standards.

Implementation Routine

As shown in Figure 5, the learner's implementation routine, "Steps for Completing a Performance Objective," is a process for the learner to follow. It is intended to let the learner manage the activity. The routine takes the learner through a simple systematic process using all the components of the package and resources. It does it without actually prescribing content or even a fixed process.

As the learner gains experience with a systematic process, it should evolve to become more and more efficient. It is important for the learner to understand from the start that there is a way to approach each new learning experience.

Our example in Figure 5 is for a structured school setting where the learner is encouraged by the people and surroundings to engage in learning activities. Even with this structure and organization, the process is needed. In the industrial O-J-T approach, it is absolutely essential that a process be included that will produce a "take charge" learner. There is very little in the work environment that encourages the learner to engage in real learning activity.

This process will vary depending on the learner, the instructional approach, and how the learning activity must be implemented. The routine is to help the student work as independently as possible while keeping on a sound learning track.

Performance Objective Checklist

Figure 6 shows the performance objective checklist. This is a complete list of all performance objectives covered in the automotive tune-up mechanic core package. The performance objective checklist serves two purposes. First, it is the student's definition of what must be accomplished in each part of the instruction. Second, it is used by the student and the instructor to judge whether or not the student achieved mastery.

Figure 5

Sample Implementation Routine

**Steps for Completing a
Performance Objective**

You are responsible for organizing and managing your own learning experiences. You have access to many resource materials and the teacher when needed. Before starting to work on this specific performance objective, be sure you understand:

- what to expect as a result of working through all the performance objectives;
- in what sequence to complete the performance objectives; and
- what resources are available to you and how to use them.

Discuss these points with your teacher before going on.

The 11 steps below are a suggested routine you should try to follow in learning to master each of the performance objectives in the program.

1. Review the performance objective, job sheet, and instruction sheets (science and math) for the objective. Identify from the instruction sheets the resources you will need. (If you have no familiarity with this performance objective, you should consider reviewing all the resources listed.)

2. Prepare a plan for using the resources and the teacher that will help you accomplish the performance objective.

3. Organize the resources to start the performance objective. Be sure facilities and materials are prepared and your teacher is scheduled to assist you.

4. Study the job sheet general information and the step-by-step procedures in preparation for doing the task.

(Continued on Next Page)

Figure 5 (Continued)

5. Start the task when you are ready. Don't hesitate to ask for assistance or to ask questions about the task. When other instruction sheets (assignment, science, and math sheets) are referenced to a step, they should be completed at that point.

6. Study instruction sheets and complete exercises as called for on the job sheet. If you cannot answer the question or work the problems, use the references noted on the instruction sheet.

7. Use the resources and references whenever you are in need of more information. Your teacher will also recommend references for you.

8. Complete the task according to the procedures on the job sheet.

9. Ask your teacher to discuss your first run through the task and give you suggestions for more study and practice as needed.

10. Study and practice until you feel you can perform a task without any aids or assistance (no job sheet).

11. Demonstrate your ability to perform a task as required and have your teacher sign your performance objective.

Ask your teacher to explain these steps to you before starting the program.

Figure 6

Example of a Performance Objective Checklist

AUTOMOTIVE ENGINE TUNE-UP

STUDENT'S NAME ....

To complete this program, you must be able to:

	DATE STARTED	DATE COMPLETED
1. Remove an automotive battery, clean battery cables, carrier, hold-down, and case with a base solution, and replace battery with correct polarity.	....	....
2. Determine strength of battery charge by testing battery water specific gravity using a hydrometer.	....	....
3. Conduct a battery and cable capacity test.	....	....
4. Test an ignition primary circuit for current flow, using a continuity tester.	....	....
5. Conduct a starting motor cranking voltage test.	....	....
6. Remove and replace a starting motor solenoid.	....	....
7. Conduct a vacuum test to identify a misfiring spark plug.	....	....

(Continued on Next Page)

Figure 6 (Continued)

	DATE STARTED	DATE COMPLETED
8. Conduct a cylinder dry and wet compression test to diagnose valve and ring condition.	....	....
9. Clean, gap, and test spark plug to manufacturer's specifications.	....	....
10. Remove and replace distributor points and condenser.	....	....
11. Set a distributor breaker point dwell to specifications.	....	....
12. Conduct a distributor advance mechanism test to specified vacuum levels and RPM.	....	....
13. Remove an ignition distributor and replace it in specified ignition timing.	....	....
14. Conduct an ignition coil test to determine leakage and shorts.	....	....
15. Test secondary ignition cable resistance.	....	....
16. Polarize an automotive generator system after component replacement.	....	....
17. Remove, inspect, replace, and adjust fan or accessory drive belts.	....	....

(Continued on Next Page)

Figure 6 (Continued)

	DATE STARTED	DATE COMPLETED
18. Determine generator output.	....	....
19. Conduct a ground test and field coil test on a generator frame with field coil windings.	....	....
20. Conduct an armature ground test, armature short test, and an armature coil balance test on a generator armature.	....	....
21. Conduct a "quick test" on a generator to determine if the generator or regulator is faulty.	....	....
22. Test a Delcotron alternator voltage and amperage output.	....	....
23. Test and adjust a Delcotron alternator regulator to specifications.	....	....
24. Test alternator diodes in the alternator.	....	....
25. Test a fuel pump for PSI pressure and volume of flow per revolution.	....	....
26. Remove and replace a fuel filter.	....	....
27. Test a PCV system.	....	....

(Continued on Next Page)

Figure 6 (Continued)

	DATE STARTED	DATE COMPLETED
28. Test and service an exhaust emission control system— General Motors A.I.R. type.	....	....
29. Adjust engine idle RPM to specifications.	....	....
30. Adjust the carburetor idle air-fuel mixture measuring intake manifold.	....	....
31. Clean and adjust a hot air type of automatic choke according to manufacturer's procedures and specifications.	....	....
32. Overhaul a carburetor to the manufacturer's specifications.	....	....
33. Test combustion efficiency by analyzing exhaust gases.	....	....
34. Remove, clean, and replace a dry element carburetor air cleaner.	....	....
35. Diagnose engine condition, using a vacuum gauge.	....	....
36. Inspect and service an exhaust manifold heat control valve.	....	....
37. Tighten cylinder heads and intake manifold to specified torque.	....	....
38. Analyze ignition operation, fuel efficiency, and valve operation using an oscilloscope.	....	....

The performance objective is written to a task which is usually something observable, so evaluation of performance can easily be judged by an expert, such as the instructor. If the performance objective is well-written, the learner will also be able to evaluate whether or not the objective was achieved. As with any objective, the definition should include standards and conditions. In the core package, these are most often specified in the specific job sheet keyed directly to the performance objective. Consequently, in programs such as this example, where instruction sheets are used, some of the standards and most of the conditions are assumed in the checklist. Only enough definition is given to be sure the learner is aware of the pieces that make up the "big picture."

Following each objective is a space for the date started and completed. For management of the activity, this can be used several ways by the learner and teacher, but usually the learner enters the start date as a reminder of the time it is taking. The instructor puts in the completion date and signature when the learner masters the objective. In some situations, there may be a time consideration. The teacher might enter both the start and completion date as a way of keeping the learner aware of the timing, as well as a way to more closely monitor the learning activity.

In a program such as our example, the sequence of objectives must be followed as it appears on the checklist. There are two reasons for this fixed sequence. First, the objectives are sequenced in order of difficulty and the logical work-flow. Second, in our example of the structured program, the instructional prompts are designed into the instruction sheets which are keyed to a specific objective; once established, the prompts are not introduced again. If, for example, the same math concept is required in, say, objectives #9, #12, and #13, the instructional prompts would only be designed into #9. In this example, taking the objectives out of sequence would make it more difficult for the learner. This core package is intentionally designed so that the ability of the student to perform one objective is dependent on the mastery of a prior objective.

As mentioned in the preceding chapter, in most on-the-job training core packages, it is not a good idea to build in the sequence dependency, unless job related. Most often, the learning experiences must be taken as they occur on the job. They cannot always be sequenced.

In the formal group class, it is often more economical to have a facility that does not require duplicate work stations for one objective, which means that each learner must be working on a different set of performance objectives in the classroom lab all at the same time.

Whether in a structured system or O-J-T, a checklist gives the student an easy overview of all those things that must be learned in order to achieve the terminal objective. It should also make the student feel that the program is in comparably small and manageable learning "bits" that, when taken one at a time, will be attainable.

The core package at this point consists of the terminal objective description, the learning process, and the performance objective checklist. In some O-J-T programs, this combination is all that is needed when the learner is put into an active and compatible work environment.

Instruction Sheets

There are several different types of instruction sheets used in the typical core package. Each is written and keyed to a specific performance objective on the checklist. Typically, the instruction sheets included in a core package would be:

1. Job sheets—one central to each performance objective.

2. Assignment sheets—one keyed to each job sheet for item identification as a "visual glossary."

3. Associated discipline sheets—any number keyed to

one job sheet to develop all required associated discipline skills and concepts.

4. Information sheets—keyed to one job sheet as a designer's "catch all" for communicating small bits of information to the learner that cannot be included otherwise, such as graphics, tables, narratives, etc.

Job Sheet

Figure 7 is the job sheet for performance objective #9 (see Figure 6, Performance Objective Checklist).

Each performance objective on the checklist has a corresponding job sheet. For the tune-up mechanic core package with the 38 performance objectives, there are also 38 corresponding job sheets.

The job sheet is prepared to be central to the learning activity which the student normally needs to master a performance objective. In terms of subject matter content, the job sheet provides only the main instructional prompts and guidance the learner will need to work through the objective. The job sheet is intentionally not written to be a totally self-contained instructional device. Other instruction and learning experiences should be needed by the learner in order to master the objective. If the job sheet is properly designed, all other instruction initiated by the learner for that objective will, however, have been stimulated by the job sheet.

Most job sheets are designed to:
- further clarify and define the objective for the learner;
- get the learner involved in the concept and knowledge needed;
- reference very specific support resources;
- set up the performance conditions by specifying tools, facilities, etc., for the objective;
- detail step-by-step procedures on priority in the performance of the task; and

- reinforce important points and stimulate further inquiry.

As each segment of this job sheet is discussed, refer back to the six segments of the job sheet in Figure 7. Segments I through VI are explained below.

I. Performance Objective. This is a restatement or slightly expanded statement of the performance objective from the checklist. The expanded statement is important because the student, when actually starting the objective, will need a more definitive statement than found on the checklist. Even here, however, a strict statement of objective conditions and standards is not needed because the job sheet itself is a detailed elaboration of the objective.

II. General Information. This segment is a brief description of the "what, why, and where" surrounding the objective. In this segment of the job sheet, the concepts and knowledge important to the performance are exposed. It is not intended to be an in-depth statement but rather just enough of an instructional prompt to get the learning process started and keep the learner headed in the right direction when accessing resources and starting the procedures.

This segment is heavily weighted by the instructional intent of the objective. If there are important associated discipline items to be learned within the performance objective, those items should be keyed to this segment. If an abstract idea is to be learned through this performance objective, then the relationships to the task should be explained, as with the example of the science and math to the gapping of a spark plug.

In an industrial O-J-T setting, the job sheet used in the core package normally contains more conceptual and theoretical information than one used in a structured, instructional school setting. Such information is much more difficult to access in the live work environment because the resource materials and people do not normally function at a concep-

Figure 7

Example of a Job Sheet

Job Sheet #9

WORK STATION # ....

NAME .... MONITORED BY ....

I. PERFORMANCE OBJECTIVE:

Given a standard used spark plug, clean, gap, and test under compression for arcing using automobile manufacturer's specifications.

II. GENERAL INFORMATION:

Spark plugs should be cleaned every 4,000-5,000 miles. Cleaned and properly-gapped spark plugs will improve engine efficiency. Inspection of plugs will indicate from color and carbon build-up the efficiency of combustion in the cylinder. The spark plug gap is critical to achieve the proper arc. An improper setting of plus or minus .005 of an inch will change the arc enough to affect engine efficiency.

III. REFERENCES:

Spark Plug Cleaning and Testing Manual
Assignment Sheet #9
Math Sheet #9
Science Sheets #9a and #9b
Crouse, *Automotive Mechanics,*
   pp. 350-353

(Continued on Next Page)

Figure 7 (Continued)

IV.   TOOLS AND EQUIPMENT:

      Spark plug cleaning machine
      Spark plug testing machine
      Spark plug manufacturer's specifications
      Wire feeler gauge
      Point file
      Solvent
      Air hose

V.   PROCEDURES:

1. Clean outside of plugs with solvent and blow air-dry.

2. Diagnose cylinder combustion from spark plug condition.

3. At the machine, select proper rubber adapter to fit plugs.
   NOTE: Sizes range from 10 to 18.

4. Place plug in adapter.

5. Apply abrasive blast to plug for about three seconds. Rotate plug slowly while cleaning.
   CAUTION: Hold plug firmly in machine and wear safety goggles to keep abrasive from getting in your eyes.

6. With plug still in adapter, give it a clean air blast to remove abrasive particles from around electrodes.

7. Clean spark plug threads with wire brush.
   NOTE: Do not brush electrodes or scratch porcelain insulator.

8. Bend outside ground electrode open to get point file under it.

(Continued on Next Page)

Figure 7 (Continued)

> NOTE: Do not bend electrode beyond opening re-
> quired to insert.

9. File both center and side electrodes to flatten surfaces.

10. Bend side ground electrode to get specified gap.

11. Measure gap using a wire gauge.
    > NOTE: Wire gauge is most accurate for this measure-
    > ment. See Math Sheet #9 and Science Sheet
    > #9a.

12. Install plug in tester finger-tight. Attach tester high voltage
    wire to the spark plug terminal.

13. Test plug firing under pressure.
    > NOTE: If plug misfires in the red or yellow range,
    > discard it. See Science Sheet #9a.

14. Test plug for air leaks along porcelain.
    > NOTE: Use few drops of oil. If there are air leaks,
    > discard plug.

15. Install new gasket on plug.
    > NOTE: If plug has tapered seat, no gasket is required.

16. Wipe outside of plug clean.

VI. REVIEW:

Select the correct response to complete statements #1–#5.
Answer questions #6–#9 where indicated, or on the reverse side
of this instruction sheet.

8   ground   3   heat range   threads   size   solvent

(Continued on Next Page)

Figure 7 (Continued)

1. Plugs should be the correct .... for the engine.

2. Clean the spark plug .... with a wire brush.

3. Bend the .... electrode to the specified gap.

4. Clean the outside of the plug with ....

5. Apply abrasive blast to plug for about .... seconds.

6. Why is the spark plug tested under pressure?

7. Why would it be beneficial to have a large gap between the center electrode and the ground electrode?

8. Which is larger, .032 or .32 or .003? ....

9. Which is a likely measurement for a spark plug, 1/250," 1/100," or 1/1600"? ....

See your instructor for the answers.

tual or theoretical level. Thus, it must be built into the package. Professional instruction and other resources found in the structured environment, on the other hand, normally do contain conceptual or theoretical information, and this need not be built into the package.

III. References. This segment of the job sheet is simply a list of references and other resources from which the learner can draw during the learning activity. This can be as specific or as general as the designer feels is appropriate for the learner. As a rule of thumb, educational programs have many open-ended references, while training programs have a few specific references.

The type of items listed here are textbooks, operator's manuals, bulletins, professional journals, films, resource people, etc. In addition, listed here are the other parts of the core package. The example in Figure 7 references an assignment sheet, two science sheets, and a math sheet. If prior performance objectives were critical to the objective, then the instruction sheets from that prior objective could be referenced also.

When the learner needs more information, there should be something listed here that will help.

These references are for support of the learning activity and not the items the learner will need to perform the specific task. If a manual is required to perform the task, then it will be included in the next segment of the job sheet.

IV. Tools and Equipment. This segment provides the learner a list of all the tools, equipment, materials, supplies, and task-specific references needed to complete the task. This list of items also serves as a partial definition of the performance objective, by specifying some of the conditions. As in our example for performance objective #9, a wire feeler gauge is specified as a tool for measuring the spark plug gap. However, because it is specified here in the job sheet, it does not appear in the performance objective statement, either on the checklist or at the top of the job sheet.

In a structured instructional situation, the facilities are organized for each specific performance objective, so some tools and equipment are assumed and not listed. In an O-J-T setting, however, the work station is not normally as clearly defined, and the learner is often required to identify and search out these items from many others. In this case, the job sheet should be very specific in this segment.

Although there may be an alternative item that will do the same job, this segment of the job sheet will only specify one.

When necessary, the tools and equipment will be referenced to or written into the step-by-step procedures in Segment V of the job sheet.

V. Procedures. This segment pulls all the programming together for the core package. These procedural steps, prescribed by the designer, are intended to lead the learner through the performance objective task. These steps should be designed to require the learner to apply all the acquired knowledge and skills previously learned to this performance objective.

The way these steps are programmed is dependent on the instructional purpose of the performance objective. In a skills program, for example, the steps would follow the exact procedures found on the job. In a core package with another instructional purpose but on the same subject, the steps, while following the same general process, could be manipulated by the designer to put more emphasis on an associated discipline item in the performance objective.

In our job sheet example in Figure 7, many of these steps for cleaning, filing, and testing are no longer practical in the real world. This performance objective, however, was programmed to teach several associated discipline items (course objectives) about electron flow and resistance. Therefore, these somewhat outdated steps were included so that several science concepts could be introduced. As long as they remain relevant to the learner and are logical to the task, they can legitimately be used as a programming device for this vocational education program. This would not be true for a skills training package.

Each step also provides the designer an opportunity to introduce information to the learner at the point where it is most relevant. Other instruction sheets specific to this performance objective are often keyed into a specific step in the procedure. As in our example, step #13 (of Figure 7) has a science sheet referenced for the learner. The information or concept to be learned from this specific science sheet is either important to the task step, or the designer anticipated the learner would be ready to use the instructional prompts at this point.

Notice in our example that each step usually starts with an action verb. These are "doing" steps, and starting each step with an action verb (when possible) provides specific direction to the learner.

The steps are intentionally short and written with as little qualifying information as possible. Added information, as suggested earlier, is isolated from the action statement. In steps #3 and #5, two examples of qualifying information are illustrated. In step #3, the information was placed under the heading of NOTE. This tells the learner that there is more to this step, but it is not the direct action required to do the step. If this separation is not made clear, the learner often loses the point of what is to be done. In step #5, the information is highlighted by the word CAUTION. This alerts the learner to information dealing with a potentially hazardous or disruptive situation. Depending on the nature of the core package subject, other "highlight" words could be used for qualifying information.

The step-by-step procedures are usually the most important part of the core package for the learner. The procedures take the learner through the task pretty much on his or her own initiative. When the learner must get assistance, the defined step becomes a specific reference point around which the learner can utilize the resources.

As can be seen in our example (Figure 7), the procedures are accompanied by a photograph. This photograph is a very detailed action illustration of the task being performed. This illustration helps the learner form an initial visual image of the task when using the job sheet.

If possible, a *photograph,* as opposed to a line drawing, is used on the *job sheet.* Line drawings are preferable for most instruction sheets, but not the job sheet. A photograph contains the detail and content to provide an impression that is helpful in orienting the learner to the task.

VI. Review. In this segment of the job sheet are questions which should help the learner pinpoint the key elements in the performance objective so that they can be reinforced. These questions should also prompt the learner to access more information and make contact with the instructor when the learner cannot respond to the questions. In most instances, the learner will look at the questions prior to working on the task. This gives the learner clues as to what to pay attention to when using resources.

If the job sheet is used in an O-J-T situation, this segment should be a very comprehensive list of questions carefully selected and written to reflect the total performance objective. When the learner is unable to respond to a question, the supervisor or some other expert can then organize and direct discussion to cover the critical, related items in the performance objective.

These questions can serve as a means for the learner and instructor to diagnose performance so that remediation can be found. The questions should not be presented as a test which is to be scored, but rather as an indicator for seeking out assistance. If the learner is properly oriented to the learning process, he or she will insist on being given more input when a deficiency is detected.

The answers to the review questions and problems can be included on the job sheet or on a separate key in the core package. In our example of a job sheet, the instructor provides the answers as a way of monitoring the learner and providing the right remediation.

In addition to the six segments discussed, the job sheet has several other important format features. At the top of the job sheet, as in our example in Figure 7, is a space for the identification number of a work station. This particular job sheet was designed for a structured learning environment where specific work areas are specified for each objective. During orientation, the student would be shown all the work stations and be asked to match the job sheet to the workplace. In O-J-T, the learner would probably identify the area by name or function.

Next is a space for the name of the person responsible for monitoring the learner's activity for the particular performance objective. The job sheet would normally be monitored by the instructor; however, other students who have mastered the task may be used. The monitoring students would not observe the learners at mastery performance. Only the instructor should judge that final performance and sign off the checklist. The same is true for an O-J-T program. In industry, a trainee is often assigned to an experienced employee who helps do the training. Even in this case, though, the trainee's supervisor should be responsible for determining qualified mastery performance.

When someone is assigned to monitor use of the job sheet, it is important to have that person actually sign the instruction sheet. This works to get more commitment from a learner. This is especially true in industry.

Both the identification of work station and the name of the person monitoring the job sheet are management devices the designer builds into the job sheet. There can be others, such as starting times, schedules of resources, frequency of assistance, etc.

The job sheet is the central device for the core package, and everything else is programmed to it. The six segments are a subset programming sequence.

Assignment Sheet

The assignment sheet illustrated in Figure 8 is an example of another type of instruction sheet.

In core packages using assignment sheets, there is usually one for each performance objective. The assignment sheet is keyed to the job sheet, as are all other instruction sheets.

In our example for performance objective #9, it is important for the student to be able to discriminate, by sight, the parts of the spark plug and to identify the parts by name. The assignment sheet is designed to prompt this development. This example has also been designed to help the learner understand the functional relationships of the parts.

Normally, the assignment sheet is one of the first learning activities engaged in by the learner when starting a new objective. It provides a reference to be used in the remainder of the learning activity.

In a sense, the assignment sheet works as a visual glossary for the student. The assignment sheet is sometimes cross-referenced to more than one job sheet when the designer feels the learner will not experience sufficient repetitions for recall or opportunities at discriminations while working on the performance objective currently being studied.

The assignment sheet has four segments, as shown in Figure 8.

I. Assignment. This segment explains the purpose of this assignment sheet. It is written to tie into the specific performance so that the learner will be sure to understand the relevance of the exercise. The statement is a description of what the learner must be able to do as a result of the exercise.

Figure 8

Example of an Assignment Sheet

Assignment Sheet #9

NAME .... DATE .... APPROVED ....

I. ASSIGNMENT:

The student will be able to identify parts of a spark plug required to clean, set gap, and test under pressure for arcing.

II. GENERAL INFORMATION:

This line drawing shows the various external parts of a spark plug. Most standard spark plugs are constructed alike. They do vary in wrench size, gap setting, and thread size.

III. REFERENCES:

Crouse, *Automotive Tune-Up,* pp. 15-16.

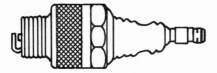

IV. INSTRUCTIONS:

1. Draw an arrow to and print the proper names of the following parts: (1) terminal, (2) insulator, (3) shell, (4) center electrode, and (5) ground electrode.

2. Draw an arrow to and initial with the letter "A" the location where the spark plug leaks compression and arcing will occur.

(Continued on Next Page)

Figure 8 (Continued)

3. Draw an arrow to and initial with the letter "B" the location where the spark will jump when properly functioning.

4. Indicate on the drawing the area which varies in size by millimeters (for different spark plugs).

5. Indicate on the drawing the area which varies in size by thousandths of an inch (for different spark plugs).

6. Indicate on the drawing the area which varies in size by fractions of an inch (for different spark plugs).

II. General Information. Much like the general information segment in the job sheet, this is intended to expose the important concepts and knowledge needed to complete the assignment sheet. It may also have an abbreviated statement to relate the assignment sheet directly to the corresponding job sheet tasks. It is assumed that more information will be required to complete the assignment sheet.

III. References. As with the job sheet, this reference segment is intended to support the completion of the assignment sheet. References should, however, be limited and very specific so that the learner does not spend any more time than necessary researching the assignment. The assignment should be tied very closely to the reference. For example, there is a specific reference for each question on the assignment sheet.

IV. Instructions. This segment contains several exercises for the learner which are directly related to the performance objective tasks. Our example asks for identification of all the parts of the spark plug which are needed to perform the task. A check of the procedural steps on the job sheet shows that both identification and discrimination will be necessary. The last question was included to be sure that the discrimination between thread size and wrench size can be made.

Although the assignment sheet is most often used for prompting the students to learn vocabulary and make visual discrimination, it can, as mentioned previously, be used to start the development of functional relationships. In our assignment sheet example, questions #2 and #3 are asked so the learner will understand what functions these parts perform and how they work together. As with all instruction sheets, there is not enough information to answer the question or solve the problem by reading only the assignment sheet. Reference resources must be utilized.

Visuals used in these types of exercises should be very

simple. The line drawing for this example of the spark plug is probably better than a photograph because it isolates and limits the image when the learner is being asked to make the initial discriminations. After this exercise, the learner will move on to the job sheet, which has a photograph, and then on to the real thing, where identification and discrimination must be more defined.

These exercises are for the learner and shouldn't be used as a test by the instructor. The teacher should, however, review the student's responses and provide confirmation and remediation as required. Some assignment sheets will provide the solutions following the problem, so that the learner can confirm some or all of the responses.

Associated Discipline Sheet

This instruction sheet is used primarily in the core package when a secondary course objective is required. In some situations, it is used to prompt course objectives within the core discipline that might require special treatment. Usually, however, the prompt for the core discipline would be programmed into the job sheet. Most often, as is apparent from the title, this instruction sheet is used to treat the associated discipline course objective. In either case, it represents one of the course objectives which is being integrated into the learner's performance objective. See the three examples in Figures 9, 10, and 11, which are part of performance objective #9.

Recall our earlier example of the integration of associated discipline items in Figures 1 and 2 of Chapter I. The three associated discipline items were shown integrated into a performance objective with the core discipline task.

These instruction sheets represent a course objective for the program's associated disciplines of science and math. Each is keyed directly to the procedures found on Job Sheet #9.

Figure 9

Example of an Associated Discipline Sheet

Science Sheet #9a

NAME .... MONITORED BY ....

I. ASSIGNMENT:

The student will understand the principle that air can conduct electrical energy and that the spark plug gap is determined in part by the factors of air conductivity.

II. GENERAL INFORMATION:

Air is commonly thought of as an electrical insulator. At high voltages, however, air becomes a rather good conductor of electrical energy. Over 10,000 volts travel through the electrodes of a spark plug. The farther apart the electrodes, the greater must be the voltage to bridge the gap. At idle speeds, the fuel mixture has relatively few particles of fuel, so that a long spark is needed to ignite the fuel. As engine speed increases, the coil output drops; however, the air fuel mixture has more particles of fuel, which helps compensate. At high speeds, the coil output drops considerably, and the spark will no longer bridge the same gap. The air gap is, therefore, set for average driving conditions.

III. REFERENCES:

Job Sheet #9
Miller, *New Science,* pp. 250-254

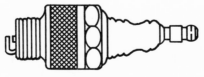

(Continued on Next Page)

Figure 9 (Continued)

IV. REVIEW:

Select the correct response to complete statements #1–#4. Answer
questions #5 and #6 on the reverse
side of this instruction sheet.

insulator   voltage   gap   conductor

1. The greater the gap, the greater the .... must be to
   bridge the gap.

2. A greater .... is needed at idle speeds.

3. At high voltages, air is a ....

4. Air is commonly thought of as an electrical ....

5. What is the effect of increasing the gap between the electrode?

6. What effect does the air fuel mixture have on the spark or
   arcing?

See your instructor for the correct answers.

Figure 10

Example of an Associated Discipline Sheet

Science Sheet #9b

NAME .... MONITORED BY ....

I.   ASSIGNMENT:

The student will understand the principle of electron flow as related to spark plug gap width.

II.   GENERAL INFORMATION:

The spark plug is designed to cause a strong high voltage electrical arc in the firing chamber which will ignite the air fuel mixture. The only time electricity will make a spark is when the electron flow must jump an air gap as it tries to get to ground.

Electrons flow with less resistance from a hot surface to a cold surface than they do from a cold to a hot surface. It requires less voltage for the center electrode of the spark plug to give off the negatively charged particles because the center electrode is hotter. In addition, the cooler ground electrode offers less resistance to current flow and, in a sense, is encouraging the electron to jump the air gap between the two electrodes.

III.   REFERENCES:

Job Sheet #9
Miller, *New Science,* p. 260

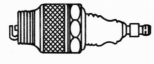

(Continued on Next Page)

Figure 10 (Continued)

IV.   REVIEW:

Select the correct response to complete statements #1–#3. Answer
question #4 on the reverse side of
this instruction sheet.

positive   hot   cold   negative

1. Electrons flow more easily from a .... to a
.... surface.

2. The center electrode is ....

3. The ground electrode is ....

4. If resistance is required to produce a high voltage arc, why is it
   important for the ground electrode to have less resistance than
   the center electrode?

See your instructor for the correct answers.

───

Figure 11

Example of an Associated Discipline Sheet

Math Sheet #9

NAME .... MONITORED BY ....

I. ASSIGNMENT:

The student will be able to compute decimal measurements required in the process to clean, gap, and test spark plug to manufacturer's specifications.

II. GENERAL INFORMATION:

Decimal measurements are used in many tune-up tasks and gapping a spark plug is one of them. Knowing decimal measurements of all types is essential to the task.

A decimal fraction is a number whose denominator is divisible by ten. Express it by place value, as shown in the following table:

$$1/10 = .1$$
$$1/100 = .01$$
$$1/1,000 = .001$$
$$1/10,000 = .0001$$

III. REFERENCES:

Job Sheet #9
Wilson, *Shop Math,* pp. 28-30

(Continued on Next Page)

Figure 11 (Continued)

IV. REVIEW:

Select the correct response to complete statements #1–#3. Answer questions #4–#6 where indicated, or on the reverse side of this instruction sheet.

twenty-five thousandths   thirty-five thousandths

thirty thousandths   forty thousandths

1. A spark plug gap of .035" is .... inches.

2. A spark plug gap of .025" is .... inches.

3. A spark plug gap of .030" is .... inches.

4. Which is the widest gap, .035, .030, or .025? ....

5. Which is the smallest gap, .035, 0.30, or 0.25? ....

6. Explain why decimal measurements are used as opposed to fractions.

See your instructor for the correct answers.

Normally, the learner would be prompted to work through these instruction sheets by the "NOTE:" on a particular job sheet procedure. In the application of the most precisely programmed job sheet, the learner would only be able to complete that step in the procedure after achieving the associated discipline course objective. More realistically, the learner will at least have some interest in the associated discipline item because it is relevant to the step being worked. In our examples, these instruction sheets will be monitored to insure their implementation.

As with the other instruction sheets, the associated discipline sheet is a prompting device and not a comprehensive instructional piece. It is made up of four segments with a format very similar to the job sheet.

I. Assignment. This segment explains the purpose of the instruction sheet and ties it into the performance objective. The more relevant this statement, the better. In some core packages, this is the "promotional" statement to interest the learner in the associated discipline item. Our examples are obviously not intended to catch the learner's attention.

II. General Information. As with the general information in the job sheet, this is intended to provide whatever content points the designer feels are necessary. As a rule, if instruction is for skills development, this segment of the associated discipline sheet would be fairly comprehensive. On the other hand, an associated discipline sheet for a general education program, with the associated course objectives as the primary intent, would rely more on prompting than a comprehensive explanation from this segment. For the latter, the program wants the learner to search out the learning activity. In either case, it is assumed more is required by the learner.

III. References. The references are intended to support the completion of the associated discipline sheet. As with the general information, the references can be as specific or general as the designer wants. In our example, which leans heavily to a skills development program, there is only one reference besides the job sheet. In this case, the one reference will provide all the information the learner will need to complete the exercises and the job sheet procedure step. For associated discipline course objectives in a general education program, there would be more open-ended references.

IV. Review. The questions in this segment of the associated discipline sheet are to help the learner identify the critical points in the associated discipline course objective. In our examples, the questions are used by the teacher to monitor and intervene in the learning activity. Because our associated discipline course objectives are very basic, the review questions are not extremely involved.

Notice that there are one or two questions at the end of the instruction sheets which will probably precipitate some discussion between the teacher and learner. The questions in all of the instruction sheets can be important for directing and managing the learner's activities as well as providing reinforcement.

In our examples, the associated discipline instruction sheets, in conjunction with the job sheet, foster the integration of the two science and one math course objectives with the core tasks of cleaning, gapping, and testing a spark plug. There will be as many associated discipline sheets per performance objective as there are associated discipline course objectives integrated into the specific performance objective.

Information Sheet

The information sheet is only used if the developer feels something important is not attainable from the existing package or from the environment. The information sheet is not an instructional sheet in the sense that has been discussed. It is not generally programmed to provide or initiate instruction.

Figure 12 is an example of an information sheet required for performance objective #9. In the school shop environment organized for the tune-up mechanic core package, there is a special work station for performance objective #9. The spark plug in the work station which will be cleaned, gapped, and tested is, however, not in a car and consequently, the manufacturer's spark plug gap specifications cannot be identified. The student can only determine the specific electrode gap by the make, model, year, and engine type.

Figure 12

Example of an Information Sheet

Tune-Up
Information Sheet #9

You have been furnished several spark plugs from different automobiles. Select one:

Champion	H10	1972 Plymouth Fury, 8 cyl.
Champion	H15	1975 Dodge Dart, 6 cyl.
AC	10	1973 Ford Mustang, 8 cyl.
Autolite	15A	1969 Ford LTD, 8 cyl.

When you have determined which automobile and engine your spark plug is from, proceed with the job sheet.

The designer, knowing the environmental constraint, prepared the information sheet which either is given to the learner or, in some cases, would be posted in the work station. In our example, the learner would select a spark plug to work on, then check the spark plug number on the chart to determine the car from which it came.

The information sheet should be used sparingly. There should not be one prepared for each performance objective, unless the core package has been developed for a discipline where there are no available reference devices or resources.

Summary

The instruction sheets are good devices for prompting and guiding the learner into and through useful learning experiences. There are no set rules for their construction, except that the instruction sheets should not be programmed too tightly. They should be designed to require the student to make decisions about what must be learned and how it will be learned.

The instruction sheet should always be obviously relevant to the performance objective, and the learner should not have to stretch his or her imagination to make the connection. In this approach, "less" is often best. The good instruction sheets will cause that "light bulb" in the learner's head to snap on frequently but only after the instruction sheet has been put away.

The four simple, straightforward components of the core package—each contributing to the organization of an efficient task-centered program—have potential in almost any education or training system.

IV.

OUTCOMES

"Since I've been taking this auto-mechanics class, my math scores are getting better."

"This is teaching . . . I help individual students when they need me. I'm interactive with the students on about 30 percent of their learning problems but that's the critical part . . . the other 70 percent they get on their own."

"I don't have trouble learning. I just can't absorb all that information you get in the classroom. When I'm in the lab, I'm always learning . . . not just trying to store information."

"Somehow it's created a different feeling between my students and me. I'm not challenging them to pay attention to the lesson, and they have stopped daring me to make them. In fact, those kind of control problems are gone."

"You know, I'm feeling more on my own. I've these jobs to do, and if I don't get them done, it's my fault. It's not easy, but I have this routine I follow and I'm doing pretty good."

"Students ask a different kind of question now. The questions are more inquiring and problem oriented."

"I'm a top student with experience in this subject. Fortunately, with this program, I can pick and choose the learning activity I need to complete my objectives."

"That new trainee sure asks good questions . . . he has a regular routine he uses for every new problem . . . some day I'm going to take a look at the training guide."

These are the typical comments associated with the uses of the core package and most other good individualized programs. What is the key to almost all these comments and what makes them different, however, is the point of relevance both in content and process. If the student can see the relevance of what is to be learned and how it is to be learned, then a whole host of positive factors can be exploited.

A partial list of the most important of those factors is:
- goal-directed learners,
- learner-relevant outcomes (accomplished),
- learner inquiry,
- learning through tasks,
- learner self-actualization,
- learner control, and
- instruction responsive to real needs.

Goal-directed learners. Students who are goal-directed learners are less tolerant of highly programmed, linear learning experiences. The core package, however, employs self-directed learning experiences. Students can pick and choose the kind of experiences they need to reach *their* goals—proceeding to learn them as they would direct themselves.

Learner-relevant outcomes. Many instructional programs are concerned with and designed for the experience of going through the program. The core package is centered on the *accomplishments to be achieved.* Such accomplishments become highly motivating influences on the students, guiding them to make progress in their learning. One institution using the essential features of a core package went so far as to specify income that could be realized by the attainment of sets of job-related objectives. The core package should always be designed around the outcomes that are relevant to the learners involved.

Learner inquiry. Many instructional experiences are a type of "spoon-feeding" exercise; not so with the core package, if properly designed. The designer must take advantage of the design components as discussed in this book, which require the learner to inquire into the learning process. This is achieved primarily through "prompting" in every learning activity. One uses prompts rather than prescriptions which specify everything that is to be done to achieve a particular outcome (objective). If ideally developed and implemented, there would be no content *per se* in the core package—only prompts. It is true that this places much of the burden on the student in the learning effort, but this is seen as a desirable need and outcome.

Learning through tasks. It has been stressed that the core package is centered around tasks. Centering learning around tasks provides a great deal of leverage, particularly in helping learners see the need to learn associated disciplines associated with these tasks. Learning concepts through tasks makes the concepts and tasks themselves highly relevant.

Learner self-actualization. In the core package, the learner not only has to follow directions (primarily as prompts), but also must invent some of his or her own processes. This helps in motivation to the extent that students can achieve objectives on their own. Also, because they do have to find their own way, students end up with a better understanding of what is involved. In turn, this provides instructional program managers (the instructor, primarily) with better insights into what is needed in the learning environment. In other words, students survey the environment and find a way within it to learn. In so doing, they tell you what is missing. The author found this particularly so when he used the core package design during Job Corps training programs. Students who had dropped out of the conventional public school environment found the core package method of learning a way to develop learning on their own terms. Many of these students came to the learning environment with better ways of achieving certain goals than the instructor could have thought of on his own.

Learner control. In general, the students using a core package design select the sequence, strategy, time to be tested, resources they will use, and so forth. These features of learner control help produce skills in decision-making, planning, use of time, and employment of resources. Rather than building in a particular program system, students must learn to deal with learning problems through a process *they* devise. Learning this process can then be generalized to a job, other courses, and life experiences.

Instruction responsive to real needs. This factor has to do with the learning environment. The environment is set up so that experts act as resources. Students use these experts on an expressed-need basis.

In closing, the design of the core package has a unique effect on the organization and administration of instruction. This is seen in the management process and environment which are tied to the instructional activities.

Much of the management process is taken off the shoulders of the instructor and used instead as part of the students' learning experience and responsibility. This is particularly important for students who have had little opportunity to learn self-management—such as was the case in Job Corps training. Certainly, this can be a difficult process for some students to undertake, but task- and goal-directed design components make self-management much easier to achieve than we might think. Using the Job Corps situation again as an example, it doesn't do much good to produce learners who can perform tasks on the job but who can't manage themselves. Taking some responsibility for their own learning management goes a long way in helping students to learn how to manage their other affairs.

V.

DEVELOPMENTAL GUIDE

Producing an efficient core package requires all the normal systematic developmental processes used to develop any other valid instructional program. There are many good routines the designer can use to perform an analysis, define course objectives, program instruction, and evaluate results. The overall process within which to develop core packages is illustrated in Figure 13.

The development of the core package, however, does require some special developmental consideration in preparing and programming the actual materials. This is especially important when the core discipline is being used primarily as an instructional vehicle to support course objectives other than core tasks.

Within the framework of the development process, as seen in Figure 13, the following seven steps for the production of the actual core package materials are recommended.

1. Prepare programming specifications.
2. Define learner's terminal objective.
3. Program performance (interim) objectives.
4. Program instruction sheets.
5. Detail learning environment.
6. Program learning routine.
7. Program implementation.

Figure 13

Development Process

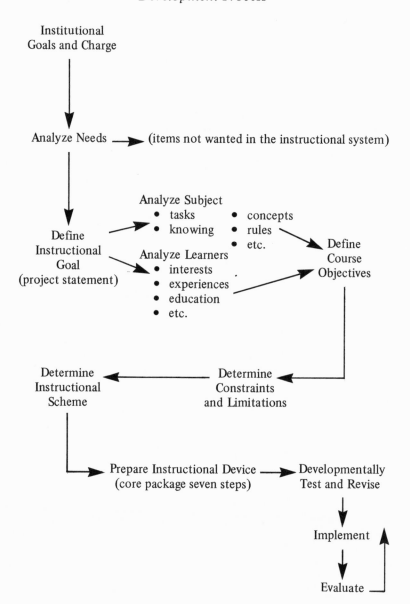

Although this is a neat sequence of steps that will fit in most development processes, keep in mind that there is always much back and forth activity in the process which normally results in small adjustments in each.

Our first step picks up after a comprehensive "front end" analysis (determination of a learning need) has been completed, course objectives have been defined, and the core package has been decided on as the instructional design.

1. Prepare Programming Specifications

After gathering all the analysis information, it is helpful to document it into a single set of specifications of important programming items. The specifications will be the designer's reference for preparing each of the core package components. The document should include both specifications and rationale for the programming.

The specifications especially important to the programming of a core package include:

a. *Instructional intent.* From a review of the institution's goals and objectives and any special charge by management, describe the purpose of the instruction and the guiding instructional philosophy for the core package. Describe how the core package will be used to achieve the institutional goals. Indicate where emphasis should be placed on the educational, vocational, and/or skills training outcomes. Identify the core discipline and how it will be used in the programming. Describe the programming needs for illustrating abstracts, establishing a skill base, and providing motivation.

b. *Course objectives.* These are the "real" objectives for the project and were identified as a result of the subject matter analysis from the existing curricula, occupational area, and/or specific job and the student population. The course objectives are a list of everything the learner must be able to do after instruction. Each course objective on this list will eventually be integrated into the learner's performance objectives in one form or another. Describe generally how the course objectives will be integrated into the core package.

c. *Constraints and limitations.* Describe items, such as budget, manpower, materials, resources, equipment, and facilities, as they affect the development and implementation of the program. This is not so much a "limiting" statement as a statement of the condition in which the core package will function. In addition, describe other conditions, such as time, attitudes, organization, and management, in the statement.

d. *Target population.* Describe the student's experiences, interests, motivations, and values. Although the subject matter is carefully accounted for, too often the *student* is assumed. With the core package, an understanding of the student may be even more important than the preparation of some other instructional program. Much of what is designed and programmed into the core package is geared to the student's interests and experiences. The programmer will go to a lot of trouble to integrate each of the performance objectives so that the course objectives are relevant to the student and match the student's ability to master the objectives. Describe how the student population's experiences, interests, motivations, and values should be reflected in the programming of the core package. Specifically, relate these to the core discipline's positive characteristics as well as this population's potential problems with the course objectives.

The programming specifications are obviously not included as a part of the core package, but they must be considered in preparing every component. It is sometimes tempting to simply rely on the results of an analysis, but this formal document forces the programmer to account for everything in a fairly detailed interpretation of the information before programming.

The specifications are also important as a reference to others. It is a means for communicating programming rationale to other managers or colleagues showing a direct relationship to the analysis information.

2. Define Learner's Terminal Objective

Using the information from the project specifications, the next step is to define the learner's terminal objective. The terminal objective should be written to reflect the learner's task-centered function after completing the program.

Recall the tune-up mechanic terminal objective in an earlier chapter. That terminal objective was written around the specific job description; however, math and science were very much a condition to successful mastery of the program terminal objective.

When the core discipline is the desired outcome, as in a skills training system, this definition is a straightforward statement of the tasks, and the integrated items are naturally identified from the task analysis of that core discipline. However, when the core discipline is not the basis for the course objective, but only a programming vehicle, then the programmer must start to integrate the associated disciplines with the core disciplines at this point.

This programming decision will affect the rest of the core package and may need to be redefined as the performance objectives and instruction sheets are programmed.

When the learner's terminal objective is defined, it should provide a very clear picture of what will be the result of instruction for the learner. It must reflect all the course objectives.

3. Program Performance (Interim) Objectives

Each of the learner's performance (interim) objectives is formed by integrating, around specific core tasks, the previously determined course objectives for (1) core specific items, such as concepts, theory, principles, rules (abstracts), and/or (2) associated disciplines related to the core task (which can also be abstracts or skills).

To write the performance objectives requires the input of well-written course objectives and a clear instructional intent. Equally important at this point are the conditions for implementation and the characteristics of the learner.

Writing these integrated task-centered performance objectives is the heart of the programming activity for the core package. Keep in mind as you prepare performance objectives that you will often need to somewhat camouflage the "real" course objective for the learner in the interest of relevance. Chapter I, Figures 1 and 2 describe the integration process.

Chances are that the sequence of performance objectives will be important to your program. All decisions about the sequence of the performance objective must be made before they are programmed.

Generally, if your instruction is directed at a skills training situation, the sequence will follow the work process. If it is directed at a vocational outcome, the sequence might follow the commonality of operations in the core discipline. If it is a general education package, the sequence might follow a chain for building the subject content. The final consideration is to have a sequence that has logic and interest for the learner and shows a clear beginning and end to the program.

As was discussed in previous chapters, the approach to this integration depends on the instructional purpose for the core package. When all the performance objectives have been programmed, they are assembled into a learner's checklist similar to the one discussed in Chapter III, Figure 5.

When your checklist is complete, you should be able to

account for every course objective in the project statement; if not, the performance objectives are incomplete. Also, when reading the learner's terminal objective, you should be able to identify one or more interim performance objectives that contribute to each item in the terminal objective. If you cannot, then the terminal objective must be adjusted to conform to the interim (or "enroute") performance objectives. The purpose of the performance objectives is to provide the learner an obviously attainable set of learning objectives leading to the desired and relevant terminal objective.

4. Program Instruction Sheets

Instruction sheets, as described in Chapter III, are used in almost all core package designs.

As mentioned in previous chapters, it is possible to have a core package without any type of instruction sheets, when the environment has been prepared to provide all the necessary prompting. In such cases, the learner, although not using instruction sheets, would use the programmed performance objectives.

A "full-blown" core package, however, will include several different types of instruction sheets. The job sheet, assignment sheet, associated discipline sheet, and information sheet were each illustrated and explained in Chapter III.

When preparing the instruction sheets, the rule is: "less is best." Remember, the instruction sheet is only a prompting device to help get the learner involved in the right activity for a specific performance objective.

How much is written into the instruction sheets depends on the learner. Whatever the designer gauges to be necessary to "activate" the learner goes into the instruction sheets. Also, the intensity of the prompts should be directed at the instructionally difficult items. "Don't kill ants with a shotgun." Each instructional entity does not necessarily deserve equal treatment. Most of the things to be learned do not require a great deal of instructional energy. A significant amount of learning can be effected with almost no instruction when the learner is in the right environment. The designer should concentrate on those things that require the most instruction.

The performance objective is the target of the instruction sheets, and each instruction sheet is written to a specific performance objective. Of the instruction sheets, the job sheet is central to the learner's activity. All other instruction sheets are written to dovetail with the job sheet procedures.

The job sheet is usually prepared first; however, as each of the various instruction sheets is programmed, it will be necessary to make adjustments.

When the associated discipline course objectives are most important, the associated discipline sheets are prepared, followed by the job sheet. These job sheets end with the step-by-step procedures as the last segment to be programmed. The step-by-step procedures in the job sheet, when written for a skills training core package, however, would probably be one of the first segments written. When preparing instruction sheets, try to start with the review questions or exercises.

Finally, the resources and references should be added to the instruction sheets after all the questions, exercises, steps, and content prompts are established.

Program the instruction sheets to the environment in which it will be implemented and to the resources available. The programmer must be careful not to put the learner into a situation where the learning activity cannot efficiently be achieved because of an improper environment.

Most of the rules and rationales for the instruction sheet segment are contained in Chapter III. All the programming will need to be carefully justified against all of the programming specifications.

5. Detail Learning Environment

This step is primarily for the structured school environment where the facility and resources are specially prepared for the learning activity. This is in comparison to the O-J-T environment, which is predictable, but not flexible. The designer normally will have taken the O-J-T environment as a given and have programmed the performance objectives and instruction sheets around the existing work station.

Even in the structured program, the core package is obviously designed with certain constraints relating to the facilities, money, materials, and manpower which go into forming the learning environment. The designer must prepare a plan that utilizes the resources to most efficiently have each learner engage in all the learning activities required to master each of the performance objectives in the core package.

It is possible to "over-build" the learning environment with what might be irrelevant resources. This can sometimes distract a learner who is engaged in independent study. Do include, however, alternative resources for most performance objectives as long as they are specific to those objectives.

Some questions to ask about the environment.

1. Is there a place in the facility for each learning activity?
2. Can the learner identify work stations for each performance objective?
3. Are there multiple examples of the performance on tape or in books?
4. Is there someone available to demonstrate the performance?
5. Are there reference materials that deal with the performance theory, concepts, rules, nomenclature, etc.?
6. Are all references listed in the core package available?
7. Is there convenient access to resources?

If the answers are affirmative, it is a good start.

6. Program Learning Routine

Prepare a procedure that will guide the learner into and through each performance objective. In previous chapters, the learner's routine has been illustrated and the rationale stated.

As with the other components of the core package, this is also designed to prompt the learner. It should provide the learner control over the learning activity and a sense of independence. The routine must obviously be compatible with the core package materials and the specified environment. It should not, however, prescribe in such minute detail as to take control from the learner. The amount of detail written into the routine depends on the designer's judgment of the learner's ability and experience with the learning process. As learners gain more experience with the core package, they become "process oriented" in their approach to learning and eventually require little or no formal direction.

The learner's routine should match the following questions:

1. Will the learner's routine get the learner to concentrate on a specific performance objective?
2. Does it get the learner to consider all the materials in the core package?
3. Does it guide the learner to prepare a plan for each objective?
4. Can the learner detect a learning deficiency?
5. Will the learner access resources to achieve competency?
6. Will the learner assume that practice is an aspect of the process?
7. Does it guide the learner to have performance monitored and seek expert feedback and remediations?

7. Program Implementation

Specifying the implementation is a programming activity as important as programming the instruction sheets. More well-designed instructional materials are judged unsatisfactory because of implementation failures than poor programming.

The management of the system must be specified. Define management routines to be sure that the learner is oriented to the system, that the learning environment is functioning, that each learner's performance is monitored, that there is coordination of learner schedules and control over learner's activity, that there is responsive interaction, that there is learner reinforcement, that there is recordkeeping, and that other such needs are going to be covered.

Your plan is dependent on the learning environment, the learners, the subject, the programming of the core package, and the institutional requirements.

After the programming steps described have been completed, the remaining development process should be carried out. Important to the program, of course, is the developmental testing and revision which will check and insure the reliability of the core package programming. The designer should review each component with several typical learners to get the learners' reactions. If learners do not respond as anticipated, the designer should revise the components after analyzing their responses.

Next, implement the core package and complete a final evaluation of the system to determine if the course objectives were, in fact, achieved and the goals of the institution fulfilled.

Finally, the development of a core package for industry can be accomplished by a trained subject matter expert or manager. Usually, however, a company training specialist will, in conjunction with the subject matter experts, prepare the package. Classroom teachers, who are familiar with programming individualized instructional material, can easily design and develop a core package. In the Appendix, there are samples from a core package which was used to train automotive teachers to develop instruction around a core package approach. The automotive tune-up examples used in Figures 3 through 12 evolved from the same core package.

VI.

RESOURCES

There are no specific texts or published references to core package design known to this author, outside of this volume. However, the following *related* materials will be useful background for teachers and trainers planning to develop core packages for individualized instruction using task-centered instruction.

Bigge, M.L. *Learning Theories for Teachers.* New York: Harper and Row Publisher, 1964.

Butler, F.C. *Instructional Systems Development for Vocational and Technical Training.* Englewood Cliffs, N.J.: Educational Technology Publications, 1973.

Fryklund, U.C. *Analysis Techniques for Instructors.* Milwaukee: Bruce Publishing Company, 1956.

Gagne, R. *The Conditions of Learning.* (Third Edition) New York: Holt, Rinehart, and Winston, 1977.

Gagne, R., and Briggs, L.J. *Principles of Instructional Design.* New York: Holt, Rinehart, and Winston, 1974.

Knowles, M.S. *The Adult Learner: A Neglected Species.* Houston: Gulf Publishing Co., 1973.

Knowles, M.S. *Self-Directed Learning.* Chicago: Association Press, Follett Publishing Company, 1975.

Langdon, D.G. *Interactive Instructional Designs for Individualized Learning.* Englewood Cliffs, N.J.: Educational Technology Publications, Inc., 1973. Chapter 6.

Mager, R.F., and K.M. Beach. *Developing Vocational Instruction*. Palo Alto, California: Fearon Publishers, Inc., 1967.

Mentzer, R.C. *System Design to Automotive Teachers Preparation*. Unpublished Masters' thesis, Chico State College, 1966.

Selvidge, R.W. *Individual Instruction Sheets*. Peoria, Illinois: Manual Arts Press, 1926.

VII.

APPENDIX

A Core Package
Development Scheme in
a Core Package Format

The following example is from a core package designed to help teachers learn to design automotive core packages. This core package was prepared for experienced auto-mechanics who had very limited teaching background. This was primarily a skills training program.

AUTOMOTIVE TEACHER
Terminal Objective

The automotive occupational teacher of job-entry-level instructional programs, who is technically prepared in automotive services and mechanical skills, will be able to plan, develop, and implement individualized learner-centered job-entry-level programs. Included will be:

1. Analysis of the occupational area to determine proficiencies, motor, and conceptual requirements for entry-level employment.

2. Specific job-entry-level learner performance objectives stated in behavioral terms.

3. Organization of equipment, tools, supplies, and facilities required by predetermined performance objectives.

4. Evaluation of existing media and development of media used with individualized instruction.

5. Determination of daily activities more effectively and efficiently as required to conduct individualized instructional programs.

The teacher interprets automotive job analysis into student performance; organizes school shop facilities for student learning; defines student objectives; provides means for student motivation; evaluates commercial teaching materials; develops automotive industrial and guidance information; organizes student activities to accomplish student performance objectives; transcribes student progress to permanent record; and accounts for supplies, tools, equipment, and materials. He or she is known by particular job accomplished; i.e., teacher, instructor, vocational automotive instructor, etc.

87

PERFORMANCE OBJECTIVE CHECKLIST

NAME ....

The teacher must be able to:	DATE STARTED	DATE COMPLETED

1. Determine the function (or purpose) of a job-entry-level automotive program by analyzing the automotive trade area and target population (student) and determining major blocks of employment suitable for target population.

          ....

2. Determine the terminal and interim job-entry-level performance objectives for a major block of instruction. These must include behavior, conditions, and standards.

          ....

3. Compile a sequenced performance objective checklist according to commonality of performance and concept complexity of performance objectives.

          ....

4. Sketch a detailed shop plan for the facilities system, laying out specific work stations according to required performance

(Continued on Next Page)

(Continued)

	DATE STARTED	DATE COMPLETED
objectives, indicating where each performance objective is to be accomplished.	....	....
5. Compile a list of all tools and equipment necessary to equip each work station so that learner will be able to complete prescribed interim performance objectives.	....	....
6. Write a job sheet for each performance objective or select commercial job sheets for student use in completing student performance objectives.	....	....
7. Select programmed individualized instructional materials to assist student in learning nomenclature and *basic* knowledge required for learner to complete performance objectives.	....	....
8. Select student operated visual devices to assist learner in developing manipulations required to complete performance objectives.	....	....
9. Determine and prepare training aids relating to learner's required performance objectives for a given number of students.	....	....

(Continued on Next Page)

(Continued)

	DATE STARTED	DATE COMPLETED
10. Determine supplies, material, and equipment needed for learner to accomplish specified performance objectives and write purchase orders with justifications based on learner objectives.	....	....
11. Prepare a student wall progress chart including all interim performance objectives condensed to job performance tasks for display in shop.	....	....
12. Organize tool storage for efficient student use at each work station accommodating all tools required for performance objectives performed at the work station.	....	....
13. Prepare, service, and operate all equipment in the shop and develop a maintenance log for each piece of equipment, including the training aids.	....	....
14. Compile an inventory of capital items, tools, supplies, and expendable items as required for administrative purposes so that every item in the shop is accounted for.	....	....

(Continued on Next Page)

(Continued)

	DATE STARTED	DATE COMPLETED
15. Compile and maintain a student file to include learner past school history and present progress.	....	....
16. Make out a daily assignment plan sheet (lesson plan) according to performance objectives and student's past learning experiences.	....	....
17. Take class roll and record attendance in conjunction with student assignment.	....	....
18. Orient students in the use of individualized instructional systems so students can use facility for learning and can identify their responsibilities to the system.	....	....
19. Give a two- or three-minute presentation for each performance objective as required by the learner to complete the performance objective when prepared media and aids are not sufficient.	....	....
20. Evaluate student progress by measuring student's changed behavior according to prescribed standards stated in the performance objective.	....	....

(Continued on Next Page)

(Continued)

	DATE STARTED	DATE COMPLETED
21. Evaluate instructional system and identify areas requiring revision as determined by student performance and industry's needs.	....	....
22. Compile and present a pre-employment package for students to simulate the job hunting and acquiring process.	....	....

JOB SHEET #1

I.   PERFORMANCE OBJECTIVE:

The teacher must be able to determine the function (or purposes) for a job-entry-level automotive program by analyzing the automotive trade area and target population (student) and determining major blocks of employment suitable for target population.

II.   MATERIALS NEEDED:

Dictionary of Occupational Titles
Employer's requirements
List of student requests

III.   GENERAL INFORMATION:

The analysis is the most important step in the preparation of instructional systems. From the analysis, you will determine everything that must be taught. Each completed analysis will differ depending on the student's desires, the employer's needs, and the facility's possibilities. Nothing outside of the employment analysis will be taught.

The analysis of the employment area and the target population is simply to find all of the characteristics of both and match them to each other. The parts that do not match, or the part of the population, become the function of the training program as it is possible within the limits of the prerequisites.

(Continued on Next Page)

(Continued)

IV. REFERENCES:

Fryklund, *Analysis Techniques for Instructors*
Corrigan and Kaufman, *Why the Instructional Systems Approach*
Dictionary of Occupational Titles

V. PROCEDURES:

A. Analyze the target population to determine:
1. Age
2. Past experiences in automotive trade
3. Reading levels
4. Formal education
5. Desired job areas of employment
6. Desired salaries
NOTE: Also include any other information about the student that you feel will assist you in determining the training program.

B. Analyze the employment area (automotive service area) to determine:
1. Different kinds of jobs available for nonexperienced.
2. Available positions in the local area.
3. Age requirements for each job.
4. Wages available for each job.
5. Educational requirements for each job.
NOTE: Types of automotive trade areas: Front End Repair, Engine Overhaul, Body & Fender Repair.

C. Match the information in A (1-6) above with the information in B (1-5) above. The more information you can account for in both analyses, the better your program will be. Hold on to all information because you may need it later.

D. Select the job areas best suited for the target population as determined by the analysis.

(Continued on Next Page)

(Continued)

>   NOTE: These areas are called Level I Automotive areas;
>   i.e., Body & Fender Repair or General Mechanics
>   or Brakes or Front End Repair, etc.

E.   Locate Level I automotive areas you selected in *Dictionary of Occupational Titles.*
>   NOTE: "Level I" automotive area is used only here and
>   not in the D.O.T.

F.   List all job classifications within the Level I automotive area.

	Brake		Level I
Brake Repairman Helper	Brake Installer	Brake Repairman	Level II

NOTE: Level II is called a major block of instruction.

JOB SHEET #2

I. PERFORMANCE OBJECTIVE:

The teacher must be able to determine the terminal and interim job-entry-level performance objectives for a major block of instruction. These must include behavior, conditions, and standards.

II. MATERIALS NEEDED:

Outline from *D.O.T.*
Employer's requirements
List of major blocks of instruction

III. GENERAL INFORMATION:

The specific interim performances that the student must be able to accomplish before he or she has completed the training program should be well-defined. The performance objectives should be considered just that, performance. When the objective is stated, it should reflect measurable behavior. The training program for "job-entry-level" skills, when analyzed, usually requires very few achievements on the part of the learner that are not expressed in a manipulation. When preparing the interim performance objectives, the instructor should keep in mind that the smaller the learning step, the easier it can be learned. Adjust the size of the learning steps by knowing the population using them.

Include these three elements in each learning objective:
a. behavior   b. conditions   c. standards

(Continued on Next Page)

(Continued)

The behavior will identify what the learner will do to demonstrate what he or she has learned. Conditions are those aiding
and/or limiting factors under which the desired behavior is to be
demonstrated. Standards define the accuracy or proficiency
which the performance must meet. All the information needed to
write the performance objectives should be in the analysis.

IV.   REFERENCES:

Mager, *Preparing Instructional Objectives*

V.   PROCEDURES:

A.   Select a major block of instruction from those determined
     in Job Sheet #1.

B.   Perform a task analysis of the major block of instruction.
     NOTE: Use technical experts and observation to deter-
            mine every task that must be performed for
            job-entry-level.

C.   Locate the job description in the *D.O.T.*

D.   Add any tasks required by the employer to the *D.O.T.*
     description, if it is not there.

E.   Delete any tasks not required by the employer for
     job-entry-level from the description.

F.   Make a statement explaining what the student (learner)
     must be able to do when he or she finishes the training
     program. That is, the student must be able to repair brake
     systems.
     NOTE: This is the terminal behavior (mission objective).

G.   Make a statement saying under what conditions he or she

(Continued on Next Page)

(Continued)

must be able to do what he or she is going to do when he or she finishes the program. That is, on American automobiles using hand tools, power tools, and shop equipment found in brake repair shops.
NOTE: This is the condition in which the terminal behavior must be performed.

H. State the amount of time, proficiency, or accuracy needed for doing what he or she is doing. That is, at the rate of speed prescribed by the flat rate manual and following the procedures as described by the manufacturer's manual.
NOTE: This is the standard of terminal behavior the student (learner) must achieve when he or she completes the program.

I. State the *terminal behavior* (objective) that the student (learner) must demonstrate when he or she completes the program. That is, the student must be able to repair brake systems on American automobiles using hand tools, power tools, and shop equipment found in brake repair shops, at the rate of speed prescribed by the flat rate manual and following the procedures as described by the manufacturer's manual.

J. List each task from your job-entry-level revised D.O.T. description. That is,
(1) remove and replace brake drum;
(2) remove and replace brake shoes; and
(3) remove and replace brake shoe wheel cylinder.

K. Check each task and determine, from your target population analysis, if these tasks as stated would make good learning steps for your students.

L. Break tasks up into smaller tasks, or learning steps, when you feel it would make it easier for the student to learn.

(Continued on Next Page)

(Continued)

        NOTE: You may add some learning steps that are not part of a job employment task but would help the learner to accomplish a task.

M.   Make a statement about each individual task, explaining what the student (learner) must be able to do when he or she finishes the task. That is, the student must be able to remove a brake drum.
     NOTE: This is the interim behavior.

N.   Make a statement saying under what conditions he or she must be able to do the task. That is, from the front wheel of a 1972 Chrysler, using pliers and 18" adjustable end wrench with the vehicle on a safety stand.
     NOTE: These are the conditions under which the behavior must be performed.

O.   State the amount of time, proficiency, or accuracy required by the student demonstrating the behavior (task). That is, in five minutes.
     NOTE: This is the standard of behavior the learner must meet for the interim objective.

P.   State the *interim objective* of performance objective by combining the results of M, N, and O. That is, the student must be able to remove a brake drum from the front wheel of a 1972 Chrysler, using pliers and 18" adjustable end wrench with the vehicle on a safety stand, in five minutes.

JOB SHEET #3

I. PERFORMANCE OBJECTIVE:

The teacher must be able to compile a sequenced performance objective checklist according to commonality of performance and concept complexity of performance objectives.

II. MATERIAL NEEDED:

Performance Objective Checklist

III. GENERAL INFORMATION:

The performance objectives are sequenced according to the difficulty that the learner may encounter in the modular area of which it is a part, and the common skills that are required for completion of the performance. The sequence of performance objectives should show the learner the logical steps to an achievable goal or terminal performance.

IV. REFERENCES:

Mager and Beach, *Developing Vocational Instruction,* p. 28.

V. PROCEDURES:

A. Separate performance objectives by modular content.
NOTE: A module is that segment of a program dealing with a specific system or type of work. Major

(Continued on Next Page)

(Continued)

Block—Brake repairman; Module—Brake adjustment; Performance Objective—Adjust shoe clearance.

B.   Arrange order of modules by the general difficulty or complexity of learning for target population.
NOTE: All the modules may be equally difficult for the learner. Refer to the past experiences of the target population.

C.   Arrange the modules of equal complexity in sequence by commonality.
NOTE: Determine the commonality of modules by the tools used and the concepts involved.

D.   Arrange each performance objective within each module by commonality of performance and the complexity of concepts.
NOTE: When concepts are linked to one another to achieve a total performance, it is necessary for them to be in sequence starting from single to multiple concepts.

JOB SHEET #4

I. **PERFORMANCE OBJECTIVE:**

The teacher must be able to sketch a detailed shop plan for the facilities system, laying out specific work stations according to required performance objectives, indicating where each performance objective is to be accomplished.

II. **TOOLS AND MATERIALS NEEDED:**

Performance Objective Checklist
Sketching equipment
Brodhead Catalog

III. **GENERAL INFORMATION:**

The facilities system should be designed using the following criteria:

1. The flow of students for progression so that the student can easily see where he or she is going next.
2. Location of tool cabinets to control student traffic.
3. Work station spacing according to performance objectives to be accomplished for safety and work.
4. Required work station duplication for heavy load areas.
5. Project storage.
6. Utilities, ventilation, lighting, etc.

(Continued on Next Page)

(Continued)

IV.　REFERENCES:

　　Guide for Planning and Equipping Industrial Arts Shops in California Schools, pp. 1-2.
　　School Shop VII.

V.　PROCEDURES:

　　A.　Determine work stations at which more than one performance objective could be accomplished.
　　　　NOTE: In most cases, if the performance objective is similar and the tools are similar, this could be considered a work station at which more than one performance objective could be completed.

　　B.　Determine the work stations.
　　　　NOTE: A work station can be bench space, stall, half carrel, etc.

　　C.　Determine arrangement and number of work stations according to the sequence of performance objectives and student load.

　　D.　Determine required storage space per work station for components and/or projects and the storage required for shop maintenance tools and extra supplies.

　　E.　Determine the space necessary for student reference and study areas.
　　　　NOTE: This may be a classroom type area or a shop study area. There may be as many as four or five in the shop. Consider location in relation to station.

　　F.　Figure the total required storage using about a six-foot clearance between bench work stations.

(Continued on Next Page)

(Continued)

NOTE: Include all *needs*: locks, storage, supplies, etc.

G.   Sketch shop plan to scale showing doors, rest rooms, and windows.

H.   Locate work stations on the plan.

I.   Locate study and reference areas.

J.   Sketch electrical and water outlets as required by work stations.

K.   Locate lights as required by work stations and according to the State of California recommendations.

L.   Sketch in the exhaust and ventilation systems as required.

M.   Number code all work stations.

N.   Make a numerical ledger listing all of the work stations and indicate the number(s) of the performance objective(s) to be completed.

RICHARD C. MENTZER is currently a Training Manager for the Equitable Life Assurance Society, New York City. In this position, he is responsible for managing the development of instructional systems for the Group Insurance Operation. Mr. Mentzer has worked as an international training consultant to government and industry. Formerly a public school teacher and Peace Corps Volunteer, Mr. Mentzer gained a great deal of design and programming experience in his work with Multi-Media Productions, Inc., Palo Alto, California, and Litton Industries, Inc.